THE PEGASUS PATROL

The History of the 1st Airborne Division
Provost Company

CORPS OF MILITARY POLICE
1942-1945

by
JACK TURNBULL
&
JOHN HAMBLETT

First published 1994

Second Revised Edition

First published in Great Britain by Tommies Guides, 2009
© 2009, Jack Turnbull and John Hamblett

All rights reserved. Apart from any use under UK copyright law no part of this publication may be reproduced, stored in a retrieval system, or transmitted, in any form or by any means, without the prior written permission of the publisher, nor be otherwise circulated in any form of binding or cover other than that in which it is published and without a similar condition being imposed on the subsequent publisher.

ISBN 978-0-9555698-9-0

Cover design by Tommies Guides
Typeset by Graham Hales, Derby

Printed and bound in Great Britain by CPI Antony Rowe,
Chippenham and Eastbourne

CONTENTS

List of Illustrations 7
Acknowledgements 9
Preface 11
Introduction 13
Foreword 15

Chapter 1   Formation and Training 19
Chapter 2   North Africa / Sicily / Italy .33
Chapter 3   A Lincolnshire Interval 65
Chapter 4   No 1 Section (1st Parachute Brigade) 79
Chapter 5   No 2 Section (4th Parachute Brigade) 99
Chapter 6   No 3 Section (1st Airlanding Brigade) 125
Chapter 7   No 4 Section (Divisional HQ) 141
Chapter 8   The Evaders & Operation Pegasus 159
Chapter 9   Prison Camps and Escapes 172
Chapter 10   The Seaborne Echelon 207
Chapter 11   After Arnhem – Norway & Denmark 216
             Roll of Honour 228
             Personal Verses 229
             Addendum 231
             Bibliography 232

Dedicated to

All Airborne Military Policemen,

past, present and future.

ILLUSTRATIONS & PHOTO ACKNOWLEDGEMENTS

Airborne Forces Museum. Pages 58, 111.
Imperial War Museum. Pages 113,114, 115, 117, 118, 166, 168
Archives Gemeindefreier Bezirk Osterheide at Oerbke. Page 169
Remainder from the Authors' own collection.

Front Cover: Lcpl J.Tofield on Security Duty at Div. HQ, Fulbeck Hall, Lincolnshire. Courtesy of Imperial War Museum.

Pegasus Airborne emblem and CMP badge, Wybo Boersma of the Airborne Museum at Oosterbeek.

Maps on pages 41 and 78 by Steve Abbott. Those on pages 86 and 146 are reproduced by kind permission of Mr John Fairley.

MAPS
Page 41   North Africa and Sicily.
Page 78   The Dropping Zones and Landing Zones.
Page 86   The Main Arnhem Bridge and Police Station.
Page 146 The Perimeter at Oosterbeek.

REPORTS
The Military Police Reports included in Chapter 2 are Crown copyright and are reproduced with the permission of the Controller of Her Majesty's Stationery Office. (PRO Ref. No. WO 1698675 XC 3184)

ACKNOWLEDGEMENTS

Gathering the information for this book took over the author's lives for a number of years and involved hundreds of letters and thousand of miles driving to interview veterans. Our homes were soon overflowing with the results of our research and we trust that we have now brought this together into an accurate and readable account.

As with all similar histories, a great many people have given their time, searched their archives, or racked their memories to provide the flesh for the bones of this story. Without them, this would have been a very slim volume indeed. Thank you.

The Staff of the Airborne Forces Museum (Duxford). The Corps of Royal Military Police Museum (Chichester). The Director and Staff of the Airborne Museum Hartenstein (Oosterbeek), Regimental Museum of The Border Regiment. Department of Printed Books at the Imperial War Museum. The National Archives. The Commonwealth War Graves Commission.

Hinrich Baumann (Fallingbostel), Irene Bishop (Claypole), Bob Bragge, Dave Brooks, David Brindley, The Reverend Joe Downing, Henk Duinhoven (Holland), John Fairley, Bob Gerritson (Holland), John Hey (Holland), Mrs Kibble, Sir John Killick, Lottie King (Claypole), A.E Hamblett, Roger King, Mrs Pawsey, Bob Peatling, Pauline Peers, Mrs B. Pell, Philip Reinders (Holland), Joe Robinson, Mike Shardlow, Joe Smith, Bill Sumpter (RMPTC), J.D. van Maris (Holland), Robert Voskuil (Holland), Mr R. Wilkinson, Fred Weatherley, Ken Wintle, Beryl Wright (Stubton).

Ex-1st Airborne Division Provost Company members – Charles 'Yoxy' Baker, Harold Bennett (Deceased), Tom 'Paddy' Breen, John 'Jack' Coates, Charles 'Charlie' Chaplin, Dennis Fitzgerald (Deceased), Bill 'Stinger' Inns, Jim 'Jock' Keddie, Harold Mason,

Richard 'Mac' McKnight, Bill Millar, John 'Jock' Mills, Jim 'Jock' Moir, George Perrott, John 'Claude' Raine (Deceased), Stan Reast, Bill 'Tosh' Richards, Dennis 'Buck' Riley (Deceased), Bert 'Junior' Stubbs, Roy Tyler, Harry Wilce, Fred Wilkinson (Deceased).

Sincere apologies if we have omitted anyone. You know that your valued contribution was most appreciated.

PREFACE

Visits to the Airborne Forces and the Royal Military Police Museums confirmed our suspicions that very little was known of the wartime role and subsequent fate of the 1st Airborne Division Provost Company. Three years of research, together with the recollections of the handful of veterans we were able to trace, will help to fill this lamentable gap in the proud history of the Airborne Forces.

Fortunately, we were able to trace members of all the Sections of the Company. Jack Coates and Jock Keddie were with the Section attached to the 1st Parachute Brigade; Jock Mills, 'Claude' Raine, 'Junior' Stubbs, 'Yoxy' Baker and Bill 'Stinger' Inns from the 4th Parachute Brigade Section. Dennis Riley, Dennis Fitzgerald and Jock Moir who were with the Section attached to Airlanding Brigade, and Paddy Breen, Harry Wilce and Stan Reast who were with Div. HQ. John Hamblett himself was the Corporal with the Provost Section which accompanied the Seaborne Element.

During our lengthy search for survivors of the Company it was sad to learn that so many veterans and friends had departed for the Big DZ in the sky, but rewarding when a name and a face from those wartime days was finally run to earth, some living in contented retirement, others still hard at work. Lengthy letters from their old Corporal, John Hamblett, together with copies of Section and Company photographs, have helped to kick-start memories and piece together names, places, and details of those days in the 1940s.

This story of the Corps of Military Police who served with the 1st Airborne Division before, during and after the Battle of Arnhem, is told through the eyes of these few proud survivors.

The Section photographs reproduced were taken at the Company Headquarters, Stubton Hall, about May or June 1944. Due to daily Police Duties, (including 24-hour Security Duty at Div. HQ), sickness and leave, a few stalwart members of the Company were absent when the pictures were taken. In addition, between that date and the Company departing for Arnhem, there were a number of inter-Section postings.

Jack Turnbull,
Marple (Cheshire),
March 1994

INTRODUCTION

This is the previously unrecorded history of the 1st Airborne Division Provost Company, Corps of Military Police. The book covers the formation of the Company in Wiltshire in 1942, its move to North Africa, the invasion of Sicily when Military Police NCOs were attached to Parachute and Air Landing Battalions, and from there into Italy. The Division's return to Lincolnshire and the long periods of inactivity and many false starts prior to the Division's heroic stand at Arnhem.

We follow the route of the Seaborne Element which preceded Operation Market-Garden in to Europe and their actions in receiving the shattered remnants of the Division as they returned from north of the river on that stormy night in late September. Finally, the story follows the re-grouping and reinforcing after Arnhem and the Operations in Norway and Denmark before the Division, and with it the Provost Company, was disbanded.

We make no apologies for concentrating on the actions of the 71 Officers and NCOs of the Company who, in September 1944, landed with the Division on the sandy heaths west of the Dutch town of Arnhem. Military Policemen who played their part, often in the unfamiliar role of infantry soldiers, throughout those eight terrible days of the battle. They found themselves in the thick of the fierce fighting sometimes armed with nothing more lethal than a Smith & Wesson .38 revolver or a Browning automatic pistol. Some in the grounds of the Hartenstein Hotel defending Divisional HQ, others at the Wolfheze cross-roads, or with the Lonsdale Force in the Oosterbeek Old Church. One Section made its way to the Main Police Station in the centre of Arnhem, while the Section Officer and one of his Corporals fought in the shattered and burning buildings beside the main road bridge.

Two of the young NCOs volunteered to remain behind on the night of 25/26th September as the battered but unbowed remnants of the Division made their escape across the swollen River Rhine. Their task was to guard the many German prisoners held in the temporary POW Cage in the Hartenstein Hotel's tennis courts. Had the guards left as the evacuation commenced the prisoners may well have raised the alarm. Their presence patrolling the outside of the wire ensured that the German prisoners suspected nothing. The two NCOs stole away in the early hours of the morning and made good their escape as they swam to the safety of the south bank.

Another group of Redcaps, led by their Section Officer and Sergeant, had the main Arnhem Police Station on Bovenbeekstraat as their objective and reached it, together with a number of enemy prisoners captured en route, on the evening of Sunday the 17th, shortly after elements of Lt. Colonel Frost's 2nd Battalion had reached the bridge. Lightly armed and with little prospect of reinforcements or re-supply, they were overrun by the enemy two days later. The Section Sergeant was killed and the remainder of the Section taken in to captivity. All, that is, except one young Lance Corporal who managed to escape. He evaded capture and crossed the Rhine some weeks later as a member of Operation Pegasus.

One NCO, attached with his Section to the 4th Parachute Brigade found himself pressed in to service as a much-needed water carrier as he sped to and fro on his motor cycle between the Brigade's position and the solitary working tap at the Wolfeheze Railway Station, festooned with water bottles. In his third such journey he was attacked by an enemy aircraft as he rode along. Despite being seriously wounded he sought cover behind a slim tree and took on a German machine gun position with his .38 revolver. Wounded a second time and with parts of his clothing on fire he was eventually captured. This is not another attempt to dissect the battle for the Bridge at Arnhem. That has already been most adequately covered in a number of excellent accounts over the years and it is not our intention to cover the same ground again. This is simply the long overdue account of a small Company of Military Policemen thrust in to a totally unfamiliar infantry role against overwhelming odds, who emerged with more than a little glory and a great deal of respect from their comrades.

FOREWORD

Years ago when training recruits I would liken Army life to a picnic – happy times occasionally, marred by a sudden downpour, which inevitably was followed by sunshine. This story you are about to read illustrates this.

The survivors of the 1st Airborne Division Provost Company, and its offshoot, 2nd (Independent) Parachute Brigade Provost Section, CMP, are now grandfathers, but behind the wrinkles and – in some cases – shining pates, lies the young Provost NCO of 60 years ago, now enjoying the fading rays of the sun.

It took a special man to become a parachutist in those early days when there was no such thing as an emergency parachute. To have simultaneously been a member of the Corps of Military Police was much more unusual; for the Corps still attracted odium surviving, mainly unjustly, from the Great War. Nevertheless we were a vital part of the Airborne organisation.

In action the Red Beret took precedence over the Red Cap, though not negating our Provost responsibilities. In back areas and bases the opposite, but we were still 'Paras'. Indeed, to the men of the Parachute battalions we were, "Our Coppers".

Personally, I count my years with the Para Provost as the best in all my service. We were a really happy band of brothers, remaining so today. Within our circle we were collectively known as 'wasters', but it is as soldiers I hope the reader will remember us after reading this excellent book. This brings vividly to life the part played by just a few men – never more than 135 – in the Second World War who, had you asked them, would have said they were only doing their bit. I think they did it very well indeed!

Major R.A.J.Tyler MBE (Retired)
(2044730 Cpl Tyler R. 1st AB Div. Pro Coy CMP)

The balloon slowly rose in to the air, creaking and rocking as it did so. I looked over the rim of the basket and watched the ground crew getting smaller and smaller, and it was then that the evil spirit of panic began to get hold of me. I gripped the edge of the basket until my knuckles were white, cursing myself for being such a bloody fool and volunteering to be a parachutist at my age.

I swung my legs in to the hole and looked up, pleadingly, at the RAF Dispatcher. My palms were sticky, my throat bone dry, and I could hear my heart pounding in my ears.

I gave a firm push forward and dropped through the hole in to space. All the fear instantly left me I as plunged towards the ground. The parachute cracked open and it was as though a giant hand had suddenly grabbed me and arrested my fall. I looked about me admiring the scenery and wondered what all the fuss had been about.

(Sgt 'Mac' McKnight remembering his days at Ringway)

CHAPTER 1

FORMATION AND TRAINING

Now who fancies throwing himself out of a perfectly serviceable aircraft?

(Airborne Provost Recruiting Sergeant. 1942)

The gleaming Willys Jeep ground to a halt in front of the wooden 'spider' office block. A cloud of summer dust rose from around the wheels and slowly drifted away in the afternoon breeze. From the Jeep stepped a tall Military Police Sergeant, to be quickly flanked by two Military Police Lane Corporals. All three wore the insignia of the new Airborne Forces on their upper arms, 'MP' armbands, boots 'bulled' to a mirror-like finish and Colt automatic pistols hanging loosely from their web belts.

The members of the Recruit squad formed up in front of the trio stared at them with a mixture of apprehension, curiosity, and not a little admiration and envy.

The Recruits formed the Senior Squad at the Corps of Military Police Depot, Mytchett Hutments, at Ash Vale near Aldershot. That very day they had completed their Police training and their ex-Brigade of Guards Instructor had marched them to the office block 'spider' for a recruiting talk by the Airborne MP Sergeant. The Sergeant vaulted effortlessly into the Jeep and turned to survey the upturned faces of the squad of new Lance Coporals:

"You've heard about the new Airborne Forces, the Paratroopers," he began, "Well, they need Military Policemen too. Only the best mind you, and you'll have some pretty stiff training to go through before you earn these." He pointed to the parachute wings which he proudly wore above his stripes. "But I can guarantee you plenty of excitement if that's what you're after, and a chance to get where the action is. There's also an extra couple of bob a day parachute pay once you've done your jumps. Now, who fancies throwing himself out of a perfectly serviceable aircraft?"

The squad remained rooted to the spot, allowing the Sergeant's words to slowly sink in. Warnings from the First World War veterans of, "Never volunteer for anything" sprang easily to mind. Others decided to opt for a quiet life and see the war through without taking any unnecessary risks.

From the front rank of the squad the tall, angular, figure of Lance Corporal John Hamblett took one pace forward. He was quickly joined by his mate from Manchester, Lance Corporal Dennis 'Buck' Riley. The Airborne Division Provost Company, Corps of Military Police, had two more recruits for its ranks. Two men who, fifty years later, would still be immensely proud to have earned and worn the Red Beret.

* * * * * * *

Recruits were attracted to join the ranks of the Company from a wide range of Corps and Regiments of the British Army. They came from a hundred different locations, and for as many different reasons. John Hamblett and Dennis Riley from a Royal Artillery Searchlight Battery not a dozen miles from their homes. Jock Keddie from the Territorial Army, (King's Own Scottish Borderers), in Scotland. Bert 'Junior' Stubbs spend the early war period with the 6th Battalion of the Lincolnshire Regiment before he was attracted to the idea of parachuting, (and the few extra bob, no doubt!) 'Yoxy' Baker had seen 7 years service with the King's Regiment on the North West Frontier before he volunteered for parachute training in India. He transferred to the Provost in 1943 as a fully trained paratrooper.

Stanley Reast had served with the Leicester and Rutland Yeomanry as a member of its Traffic Control Company. It was probably due to this tenuous link with things 'Police' that he found himself suddenly transferred to CMP and posted to Tunbridge Wells in Kent. Returning from a Police Foot Patrol around the town with an empty notebook he informed his Officer that he couldn't see what reporting soldiers for not saluting had to do with winning the war! That earned him 7 days Confined to Barracks and a suggestion from his Sergeant Major that the best place for him would be the front line. Shortly afterwards Stan joined the Airborne Provost.

Acting/Unpaid/Lance Corporal Harry Wilce was serving with the RASC in Hooge Lines, Catterick. Whilst on leave in London he was attracted by a Military Police Recruiting stand set up in Selfridges store. Two smart MPs stood beside their gleaming motor cycles on the stand. Harry was wearing his civilian clothes and listened patiently to the NCO's recruiting 'patter', then gave them his home address thinking that a career in the CMP might be beneficial when hostilities had ended. When he returned to Catterick he also paid a visit to the Officer in Charge of the Police unit there. In the time honoured army fashion – he heard no more about it! Some months later his unit was warned for overseas service and Harry's Sergeant Major sent for him. In one hand he held a 7 day Embarkation Leave pass, and in the other Harry's application for transfer to Provost. "Which one do you want?" asked the Sergeant Major. There was only one choice! Harry went on leave. Later, after the move overseas had been inexplicably cancelled, Harry moved to Kent as a driver at CRASC HQ. He hadn't been there very long when his transfer to CMP came through – as a result of his chat with the MPs in Selfridges. At the end of his Police Training he was attracted by the thought of …. "Seven days leave on completing the parachute course." Together with his pal Paddy Breen he joined the Airborne CMP.

Bill 'Stinger' Inns served as a Machine Gunner with the Durham Light Infantry before being sent to Orkney in charge of a squad operating experimental guns. He remembers "There wasn't a woman, there wasn't a tree, and there wasn't a pub. The men used to go around doing the Seagull Dance. That was hopping about on one leg and squawking like a seagull. That place really got to you." His application for transfer to the CMP was finally accepted and, with a sigh of relief at escaping the boredom, he travelled down to Mytchett for his training. Lance Corporal Roy Tyler, after numerous attempts, managed to obtain his transfer from the Somerset Light Infantry to the CMP two weeks after his 21st Birthday. Within a further 5 weeks he had completed Provost training, volunteered for the Airborne CMP, qualified as a parachutist, enjoyed 5 days Embarkation Leave, been thrown in to the river at Salisbury by anti-social paratroopers, and sailed from Scotland bound for North Africa. The experiences must have been somewhat to his liking because he remained with the Corps for the next 33 years until he finally retired in 1976.

Others to join the Company, like Jack Coates, John 'Claude' Raine and Dennis Fitzgerald, who were to feature prominently in the activities of the Company over the next couple of years, came to Provost direct from the Parachute Regiment. Their experience was but one of the ingredients which helped to form the many individuals in to a cohesive unit.

On the 10th October 1941 the 31st Independent Brigade Group, a formation of Regular troops with service in India, was converted to the role of an Airlanding Brigade Group. It was anticipated that the Brigade would be transported to a war zone either in gliders or in aircraft which would land on a suitable airfield or level strip of land. For this reason they were to be known as 'Airlanding' and not 'Gliderborne' troops. This formation was re-named 1st Airlanding Brigade Group and included a Provost Section which was based at 'B' Camp, Barton Stacey.

Before the end of the year the Provost Section came under the control of the newly-formed Airborne Division and at a conference held at Airborne Division HQ in February 1942 it was proposed that the Provost establishment be increased to six Sections. Recruiting began in earnest to raise the additional five Sections. In April 1942 the existing Section was on the move again, this time to Holme Farm, Stockcross near Newbury.

The following month Airborne Division Instruction number 6 stated that, in the event of an enemy invasion of England, the allotment of the Provost would be; 2 Sections to 1st Airlanding Brigade, 1 Section to 1st Parachute Brigade, 1 Section to Div. HQ with the remainder being held in Div. Reserve.

In June 1942 Divisional Location Statement Number 4 had the Section packing its bags yet again and moving to Beacon Barracks at Bulford. By August, and Location Statement Number 5, recruiting must have been proving successful because the 'Section' became a 'Company' and was to be known as the Airborne Division Provost Company. The title was prefixed by '1st' before the Company sailed for North Africa the following April.

The first place that the Company could really call 'Home' was at the old Beacon Barracks in Bulford, and it was to there that the new arrivals came. The transfers from their respective units, and the new recruits direct from the CMP Depot at Mytchett. John Hamblett remembers his arrival at Bulford well. He was taken straight to the Dining Hall for a huge meal of braised steak .... "To build you up for the hard training to come."... Then in to a long, wooden hut which was .... "Dark, smelly and overcrowded, with a large coke fire burning in the centre of the hut. Snores and grunts greeted me as I stumbled around in the dark trying to find a spare bed."

At that time the CMP did not have its own Corps of Officers and Provost Officers were selected from other Corps and Regiments. The Officer Commanding the new Company was Captain O. P. Haig of the Ox and Bucks Light Infantry, and a member of the famous whisky family. Together with a brace of immaculately turned out NCOs proudly sporting their Airborne insignia and parachute wings he often toured the Military Police units in the South of England on a recruiting drive. Their routine was to arrive in a 'bulled-up' Jeep, park in a prominent spot within the CMP unit lines and soon the inquisitive and curious Redcaps would surround the vehicle. It was reminiscent of the Redcoats and the peripatetic Recruiting Sergeants. Many of those NCOs who took part in the airborne invasion of Sicily and who later fought and died in the horrors of Arnhem were to join the Company in this way.

One of these early recruiting visits was paid to the CMP Depot in an effort to entice a number of the Instructors there to join the Company and try for the coveted Red Beret and the parachute wings. Amongst those who followed Captain Haig and his NCOs back to Bulford was Sergeant 'Mac' McKnight, late of the Scots Guards, who was to become the 'father-figure' of the Company as he instructed the young NCOs in the intricacies of Policework and Foot Drill. Another Instructor to join from the Depot was CSM Jock Gray. This one-time Liverpool Policeman was to be the Company's first RSM before being commissioned and eventually assuming command of the Company in time to lead it in to Arnhem. Sadly, he was never to see the streets of his beloved Liverpool again. Sergeant Bill Kibble, also an Instructor at the Depot and a pre-war Grenadier Guardsman, would follow Jock Gray as RSM of the Company and end the war as a prisoner in Stalag XIB at Fallingbostel. There he became the right-hand man to RSM John Lord of 3rd Parachute Battalion who was also a pre-war Grenadier.

In the wooden huts of Bulford the new arrivals who had not passed through the CMP Depot were introduced to the mysteries of Police Procedures, Escort Duties, the Recording of Statements and the writing of the (infamous) Army Forms Blank 252. Those NCOs who had transferred from other CMP Companies, and who were already trained in the various aspects of Policework, filled their time waiting to go for parachute training with security Duties at Div. HQ, Traffic Duties and Foot and Mobile Patrols of the nearly towns and hostelries.

Fitness training was also very high on the agenda and took up much of the NCO's time at Bulford. Early morning road runs would be enlivened by a lung-bursting run up and down one of the many hills with the half-awake squad staggering beneath the weight of a telegraph pole on their shoulders. Then it was in to the Bulford Camp Gymnasium under the eagle eye, and rippling muscles, of a PT instructor who would take a sadistic delight in putting these fledgling coppers through his torturous exercises. John Hamblett had vivid memories of … "Countless rounds of milling in the boxing ring trying to belt the hell out of each other wearing huge padded boxing gloves."

Gradually the new Company was being moulded in to shape ready to take its place in the Airborne Division. Leadership of the highest quality came from the Senior NCOs, many of whom came originally from the Brigade of Guards and were experienced pre-war soldiers. Others had a Civil Police background and brought their knowledge and experience in to the classroom. The Section

Officers on attachment to the Company came mainly from the Parachute Regiment, or from the Regiments making up the Airlanding Brigade. Again, they brought leadership of a very high standard. The young NCOs, all eager volunteers, responded to the challenge and it was not long before the Company displayed that bond of comradeship that esprit de corps so essential for what lay ahead.

And then it was on to Hardwick Hall, not far from Chesterfield, for fitness training and the introduction to parachuting. The new arrivals were accommodated in huts in the grounds of the Hall, fortunately close to a footpath leading to the village of Doe Lea and the Working Men's Club. The 16th Century Hardwick Hall had been the elegant home of the Countess of Shrewsbury, but now its walls and manicured lawns echoed to the grunts and groans of countless would-be paratroopers.

The first fourteen days of parachute training were spent at Hardwick where Officers, NCOs and Private soldiers were treated equally. They all had to double everywhere. Double to the Parade Ground, double to lectures, double to meals. Everything was done at the double, from morning 'til night. Those first two weeks were to test to the limit the men's mental and physical qualities and to ensure their total suitability for parachute training. This was the sorting-out period, and there were certainly failures. Some through accidents or injuries sustained during the strenuous exercises the volunteers were put through. Others decided that they couldn't attain the high level of fitness and commitment required of them. In either case they were quickly returned to their original units.

As Lance Corporal Harry Wilce remembers.... "We arrived at Hardwick Hall and were housed in huts in the Hall grounds. We were formed in to 'sticks' of 10 men with no priority or preferential treatment for the Officers, and from then on it was jog-trot all day long. From First Parade to knocking off time it was all done at the double. The camp was built on a steep slope which was OK after Roll Call when we had to double to the mock-up fuselage, but pretty hard going at the end of the day running back up the slope to be dismissed."

Lance Corporal Bill Inns had a tougher time than most at Hardwick. When he arrived for his two weeks training he found that his brother was an Instructor there. Not only did he ensure that Bill passed the course, but that he was in the best possible physical condition at the end of it. Where everyone else had to do something once, Bill had to do it two, and sometimes three times.

Once the sorting out and toughening up period at Hardwick Hall ended the survivors were marched to Chesterfield Railway Station for the next phase of their parachute training. This would take place at Ringway near Manchester. Here they would complete a number of parachute descents both from a static, tethered balloon, and from an aircraft. Only then would they qualify for the coveted 'Wings' and the right to wear the Red Beret.

In the early 1940s not only were the volunteers complete strangers to parachuting, they were also strangers to flying. Charter flights to exotic holiday destinations for the masses were a thing of the future. Few had been up in the air at parachuting height and had the experience of looking down to see the features on the ground appearing in miniature. Now, not only were they to be taken up to that height, but they were going to be ordered to leap in to space and trust their lives to 'chutes packed for them by a complete stranger.

Ringway had been selected as the parachute training centre in the summer of 1940 when the Prime Minister, Mr Winston Churchill, had ordered the formation of ….."A Corps of at least 5,000 parachute troops." The original military designation for Ringway was, The Central Landing School, but after mail began to arrive addressed to, 'The Central Laundry' and 'The Central Sunday School', the name was changed and it eventually became simply, 'The Parachute Training School, Ringway'.

The training at Ringway included 'synthetic' ground training to simulate conditions which the paratrooper would encounter in the air. Some such simulators had been rushed in to wartime service without the advantage of adequate testing and fine tuning which the inventor may have wished for. Sprains, fractures, twisted ankles and knees meant that the device was rapidly abandoned. As was the practice of leaping from the tailboard of moving lorries to simulate a parachute landing. One hangar at Ringway housed mock-ups of the fuselages of Whitleys, Dakotas and Halifaxes, through the doors and apertures of which the trainees practised their exits and landing positions. Feet and knees together, soles of the feet parallel to the ground, and the method of collapsing the body on the ground known as the 'parachute roll'. This absorbed the speed of drift and the shock of falling. Once perfected it was hoped that the trained paratrooper would be able to make a safe landing either forwards, backwards or sideways at speeds up to 20 mph.

Another hangar contained a variety of swings, trapezes and slides to assist in the training. One piece of equipment, still used in the training of parachutists today, was known as 'The Fan'. This was a device which allowed a man to jump from a height of 25 feet with his harness attached by cable to a steel drum. His speed of descent was controlled by a spinning fan and he landed with the same force as if he had jumped by parachute.

Whatever mechanical or man-made contraptions were provided to prepare the trainee for parachuting, there was nothing which could prepare him fully for his first jump, or drop, from the tethered balloon. It was, without doubt, a most memorable and frightening event. As Dennis Riley was to remark some 50 years later …"The second most exciting experience of my life!" … The slow ascent sitting in the flimsy basket suspended beneath the sliver grey balloon. The gentle swaying motion and the eerie silence as the figures on the ground slowing receded. The basket carried the four trainees and a Royal Air Force Instructor. Exit from the basket was through a hole in the floor, one at a time, on the barked orders of the Instructor. Sergeant 'Mac' McKnight remembers it this way:

> *After all these years that first jump is etched on my brain and will forever haunt me. Four of us were detailed for the first drop, two Corporals, a Lieutenant and myself. We took our places in the basket, seated on the floor, and accompanied by the Dispatcher. He was an RAF Sergeant and would give the orders to jump. He stood astride the hole in the floor of the basket, checking that the static line of each parachute was secured, then gave the order to the ground crew to winch up the balloon.*
>
> *The balloon slowly rose in to the air, creaking and rocking as it did so. At about 2 or 3 hundred feet I looked over the rim of the basket and saw the ground crew getting smaller and*

smaller. It was then that the evil spirit of panic began to get hold of me. I gripped the edge of the basket until my knuckles were white, cursing myself for being such a bloody fool and volunteering to be a parachutist at my age.

We reached to jumping height and the basket jerked to a halt. The Dispatcher shouted "Take up position Number 1"....One of the Corporals swung his legs in to the hole keeping his eyes fixed on the Dispatcher. The Dispatcher said ... "When I shout GO!, you go"....

The Corporal nodded. Seconds later there was the command... "GO!"...The Corporal pushed himself forward and disappeared through the hole and plummeted earthwards. This caused the basket to rock violently and I took a firmer grip on the rim. Two minutes later and Corporal number two repeated the process.

Number 3, the Lieutenant, took up his position and, looking at this face, it was a toss-up which one of us was the most scared. On the command ... "GO!" ... he feebly tried to push himself forward through the hole. He didn't go. The Dispatcher glared down at him and said, ... "Sir, I will only say it once again, and this time I want you to make a good exit. Understand?" .... On the next command... "GO!".... the Lieutenant disappeared through the hole. And then it was me.

I swung my legs in to the hole and looked up, pleadingly, at the Dispatcher. My palms were sticky, my throat bone dry, and I could hear my heart pounding in my ears. I felt physically sick. The RAF Dispatcher looked at me and grinned. He said, "I know I won't have any trouble with you Sergeant, because I know you wouldn't want to return as a failure to your unit"...I gave him a weak, sickly grin and nodded, silently mumbling a prayer to myself. The thought of a Roman Candle flashed through my mind in the split second before the Dispatcher yelled...."GO!"

I gave a firm push forward and dropped through the hole in to space. All the fear instantly left me as I plunged towards the ground. The parachute cracked open and it was as though a giant hand had suddenly grabbed me and arrested *my downward fall. I looked around me admiring the scenery and wondering what all the fuss had been about, then a voice boomed up at me through an amplified speaker on the ground.. "Watch your drift Number 4"... I looked down and saw that the ground was rushing past the wrong way for a good landing. I hit the ground with an almighty thump and lay there in a crumpled heap for a second or two. I was down and all in one piece. Nothing broken and nothing missing. As someone once said "If you can get up and walk away, it's a good landing". I think the same person also said:*

> *'Jumping through the hole*
> *Jumping through the hole*
> *I'll always keep my trousers clean*
> *When jumping through the hole'*

Harry Wilce kept his eyes tightly closed on his first balloon jump, only opening them at the last minute before he hit the ground. He thought that he had made a hash of it, but Ground Control complimented him on his descent and good landing. He gathered up his 'chute and walked over towards his mates ... "It's OK nothing to it . Just like jumping off a wall".... On his second jump he was detailed Number 4. Numbers 1 and 2 left the basket in their turn and then the Dispatcher yelled... "Number 3 GO!"....Harry swung his legs in to the hole ready for his turn only to discover that Number 3 was still sitting opposite him.

The Dispatcher said... "Ready Number 4, I'm going to push him off" ...With a bit of assistance from the Dispatcher Number 3 eventually left the basket. And then it was Harry's turn. He was falling, falling, 120 feet before the canopy 'plopped' open. Harry looked down and saw the front of his jumping smock was covered in blood. He remembers:

I hit the ground like a bag of you know what, legs wide apart, and crashed onto my back. I came to in Tatton Park Blood Wagon, (the MO's Station Pick-Up Truck), and was rushed to the First Aid Post where they stitched up the gash under my nose. With the bits of stitches hanging down I looked like

> *a whiskered cat. I thought that I had 'Rung the Bell', but apparently I had left the balloon as the Dispatcher was hauling in an empty parachute bag and the metal hook had smacked me under the nose.*

Balloon jumps completed and it was now time for the real thing – five jumps from the twin engined Whitley. This was a converted bomber with an aperture in the floor at the rear of the fuselage through which the paratroopers had to exit the aircraft. Those about to jump sat on the floor of the aircraft, legs straight and facing in alternate directions. On the command of the RAF instructor the first to drop swung his legs in to the hole and gripped the sides tightly. As he dropped in to space the rest of the trainees shuffled along the floor towards the hole. The idea was to push off, assume the position of attention, and drop neatly through the hole towards terra firma, which was not an easy thing to accomplish when laden with equipment. Push too hard and you hit the opposite side of the hole. Not hard enough and the parachute pack worn on the back would tilt you forward onto the far side of the hole. Either way the result was a broken nose or the loss of a couple of front teeth. The practice known as 'Ringing the Bell' would also cost the unfortunate man a round of drinks for the other members of the stick.

The wartime parachute canopy was made either of nylon or cotton and was twenty eight feet in diameter. In the centre was a circular hole twenty two inches in diameter, this was to allow some of the trapped air to escape and prevent undue strain on the canopy when it opened. The rigging lines attaching the canopy to the harness worn by the parachutist were twenty two feet long. The life of the man leaping in to space, from an aircraft or from a balloon, was in the hands of the parachute packer. These were mainly ladies of the Women's Auxiliary Air Force who were all highly trained experts and would spend, on average, twenty-five minutes inspecting and packing each 'chute. Once brought in to service each canopy would only be used for a maximum twenty-five descents.

At all times the paratrooper used a 'statichute'. This was operated by a static line, a length of webbing about twelve feet long with a snap hook at one end. The other end of the static line was secured to the parachute bag. Before jumping the paratrooper hooked the static line to a cable inside the aircraft and this ensured that the parachute was automatically operated once he had fallen the length of the webbing. The static line would pull the bag off the parachute allowing it to fill with air.

The clothing worn by the would-be paratrooper was designed to give him the maximum warmth in the air, and the maximum mobility once he was on the ground. On top of his normal battledress would be his camouflaged parachute smock, made of windproof material and with large pockets. His webbing equipment would then be fitted over the smock. To prevent his parachute rigging lines from snagging on the webbing equipment he put on a loose fitting jumping jacket. Finally, his parachute harness was fitted. In the early days of the war the paratrooper was issued with thick rubber-soled boots, but that was later found unnecessary and ordinary army issue boots were worn. For practice jumps the helmet used can best be described as like a flat, circular cheese. But for operations the familiar rimless steel helmet was worn.

Understandably, the obligatory descents from the aircraft are not remembered as vividly as those first ones from the balloon. What **is** remembered is the smell of the aircraft and the deafening noise of the engines with the slight change in pitch as the aircraft approached the DZ. The Dropping Zone for the trainees of Ringway was Tatton Park, just a few minutes flying time away out in the Cheshire countryside. Plenty of open space in the extensive parklands around Tatton Hall, but also plenty of trees and a couple of lakes waiting for the unwary paratroopers.

The trainees grouped in to sticks of ten men for the aircraft jumps which started with them dropping in pairs at a slow pace. The pace and size of group was increased until, on the final drop, the whole stick left the aircraft as rapidly as possible. The closer they could exit from the aircraft, the closer together the stick would be on the DZ ready to group and go in to action.

Leaving an aircraft travelling at around 100 mph was like nothing the men had experienced before. Once clear of the aperture they were whisked away by the aircraft's slipstream as though grabbed by a giant hand. In an instant the static line had snapped taut, dragging the bag from around the parachute and leaving the trainee suspended beneath that beautiful, reassuring circle of silk. There were a few seconds of relief, peace and tranquillity before the Instructor on the ground could be heard yelling up to him… "Good exit Number 1. Now keep your feet together, you won't lose anything"… Then he hit the ground. Knees and feet together, in to a perfect parachute roll, hit the metal box on his chest to release the parachute, then gather in the 'chute ready for the next jump.

Soon the five aircraft jumps were behind them and it was Wings Day. This was the culmination of, possibly, the toughest and most demanding period of the Airborne Military Policeman's life. It was also a day he would long remember with pride in his own personal achievement. At any time up until now he could have changed his mind. Packed his kit and gone off to some cushy billet with a more sedentary Provost Company where he could keep his feet firmly on the ground. Where he would not be expected to maintain the highest level of physical fitness, dedication and commitment expected of him as an Airborne soldier. But now, once he accepted those coveted Wings, a refusal to jump when ordered to do so would most probably result in a severe custodial sentence, not to mention the ignominy of being returned to his original unit.

And then it was back to Company HQ at Bulford. It was October 1942 and the 1st Parachute Brigade was soon to depart for an unspecified destination. Roy Tyler, Paddy Breen, 'Stinger' Inns, John Hamblett, 'Charlie' Chaplin and the rest of the newly trained Airborne Military Policemen were about to get their knees brown.

CHAPTER 2

NORTH AFRICA, SICILY AND ITALY

We had been dropped on the wrong DZ and were in the middle of a well defended enemy location.

(Sgt. 'Cab' Calloway after the invasion of Sicily)

Training for the Company's role within the Division continued throughout the winter of 1942/43, with scant regard for the harsh weather experienced on Salisbury Plain. Police Patrols and Security Duties at Div. HQ were interspersed with sessions of fitness and weapon training. More recruits arrived and were quickly processed through the Hardwick Hall and Ringway parachute training systems to return to Bulford leaner, fitter, and occasionally minus the odd front tooth courtesy of 'The Whitley Kiss'.

Those NCOs detailed for the Provost Section attached to the 1st Airlanding Brigade operated from Larkhill from where they carried out their Security Duties and Town Patrols. Their training included practising loading and unloading vehicles and trailers from gliders, plus the occasional familiarisation flight. Although they were attached to the Airlanding Brigade they were also required to complete the full parachute training in order that, should the need arise, they could be posted inter-Section within the Company.

January 1943 opened with half the Company being sent back to the CMP Depot at Mytchett for a Battle Course and infantry training, plus a brush-up on their Police Procedures. The second half of the Company went to Mytchett in mid February but the course was cut short when the Company was warned for an imminent move overseas. John Hamblett was a keen rugby player and the unexpected return to Bulford cost him his place in the Aldershot Services Team to play the Royal Navy (Chatham) on the following Saturday.

In an attempt to hide the impending overseas destination of the Company (and the Division), from inquisitive eyes around Bulford, NCOs collected their KD (Khaki Drill), desert clothing from the Quartermaster's Store and secreted the shorts, shirts, puttees etc., inside a kitbag before returning to their billets. They were also warned of the dangers of indiscreet conversation in the local pubs or in letters home. The cover was well and truly blown when one of the Larkhill Section's wooden huts was burnt to the ground in a mysterious fire. All that remained, for the world to see, was the pot bellied stove, still with a tray of finnan haddock in milk resting on top of it, and the KD clothing scattered around outside on the grass. (At least one veteran has hinted at suspicious goings on by the Q Stores staff, and that a great many of the Company records went up in smoke along with the hut!).

In early November 1942 the 1st Parachute Brigade had left Bulford for North Africa as part of Operation Torch, a combined amphibious and airborne assault on French North West Africa. The objective being to occupy Tunisia before the retreating German Army could establish itself there, and also to gain the support of the French population. The Brigade comprised the 1st, 2nd, and 3rd Battalions of the newly formed Parachute Regiment, together with units from the Royal Engineers, Royal Signals, and the Royal Army Medical Corps, but with no Provost section. The remainder of the Division, the Airlanding Brigade, 2nd Parachute Brigade and the supporting troops were to follow them to North Africa in the spring in preparation for the forthcoming invasion of Europe through Sicily and Italy.

Half of the Provost Company were to accompany the Division, with the remainder following at the end of May. A handful of NCOs were to be left behind to form the nucleus of the 6th Airborne Division Provost Company. Farewells were said to the ladies of Bulford late at night on the 12th April and the party travelled by train up to Gourock in Scotland. Two days later the Division was in a convoy heading down the Clyde in to an unknown future. Harry

Wilce remembers the vessel which carried the Provost Company as being.... "A Dutch ship, captured by the Germans and re-captured by the British, with a Javanese crew and a Dutch Captain who was violently sea-sick each time the ship left port".

The ship docked at Oran in Algeria on the evening of 22nd April 1943 and the Company were loaded aboard US Army lorries for the 50 mile journey inland to the village of Tizi, a few miles from Mascara. The trucks were driven at breakneck speed by grinning American Negro soldiers, mouths full of chewing gum and teeth clamped firmly around a fat cigar. The hair-raising journey over the mountains is remembered vividly by all those veterans we spoke to, with the exception of Stan Reast who managed to sleep throughout the whole journey.

A number of NCOs followed along behind on the Company's motorcycles, losing various bits off their machines en route as the rough desert roads and tight mountain bends took their toll on the nuts and bolts. John Hamblett finished the journey some days after the main party, much to the RSMs displeasure, after he had stopped to help Dennis Riley and 'Busty' Edwards whose machine had lost too many bits. John had to tow the two crippled machines with his own to a friendly RAF Station for emergency repairs before continuing the journey.

The first few days at Tizi were spent as guests of the US Army. The accommodation was under canvas in tents erected to house anticipated Prisoners of War. Unfortunately, the tents had been pitched in a shallow wadi and a terrific thunderstorm soon turned the wadi in to a raging torrent. The next morning the barbed wire fence surrounding the camp was festooned with drying tents and various items of personal clothing. Meanwhile, Reconnaissance Patrols of the surrounding area were sent out, one of their main objectives being to find more suitable accommodation for the Company. Within a week this was found in the form of a large garage down the road in Mascara and by the 6th May Company HQ and all the Sections were settled in there.

On the instructions of Div. HQ all Arab quarters were placed Out of Bounds and the Company was tasked to provide Traffic Pointsmen and Patrols of Mascara and the surrounding district. Dress for duties was KD uniform with MP armband and peaked cap worn with the familiar red cap cover. The NCOs wore the parachute wings on their sleeve which proved rather difficult to spot when involved with a crowd of brawling Paras in a bar. The feeling was that the Red Beret would have afforded a greater degree of protection from, and acceptance by, the other members of the Division. But the General had the last word and **he** wanted his Redcaps to wear the peaked cap!

The months of May and June were a settling in and acclimatisation period. Security and Patrol Duties took up much of the time, but there was also a considerable amount of training to be done for the impending assault across the Mediterranean in to Italy. The Americans had supplied Douglas C47 (Dakota) aircraft to replace the familiar British Whitley bombers on which the Division had trained at Ringway. Exit from the Dakota for the paratroopers was via a side door, a vast improvement from the hole in the floor of the Whitley, but required familiarisation flights and drops to be completed. In addition, for the operations to be launched from North Africa the HORSA gliders used by the Airlanding Brigade in training in England had to be replaced by the much smaller American WACO, (also known as the HADRIAN). A valiant attempt was made to tow a number of HORSA gliders the 1,400 miles from England, but in the event only a very small number were made available. The Airlanding Brigade and its Provost Section had therefore to acquaint themselves with the loading and unloading problems of the WACO in readiness for the forthcoming operations.

Following the arrival of the Company Rear Party from England on the 27th May, the strength of the Company stood at; 3 Officers, 1 Warrant Officer, (RSM Jock Gray), plus 122 NCOs and Other Ranks. Of this total the 3 Officers, the RSM and 83 NCOs were fully qualified parachutists. The Officer Commanding the Company was Captain K.G.Wells, Captain Haig having been promoted to Major before the departure from England and assuming the appointment of Assistant Provost Marshal at Div. HQ.

June 1943 was a busy month for the Company, and indeed the Division. There was a great deal of activity with flights and simulated or actual jumps from the unfamiliar Dakotas. The paratroopers soon came to appreciate the relative comfort of the

American aircraft compared to the Whitley. It was far larger inside with room for them to move around, stretch their legs, and exit through the side door without fear of 'Ringing the Bell'. Once the initial teething problems had been resolved exits became much faster, easier and safer. During the month there were 13 NCOs who arrived at the Company but who decided that leaping out of an aircraft, regardless of its 'comfort' was not for them and they were posted to spend their war in a more sedentary Military Police unit.

Second Lieutenant Gus Risman, who had been a Physical Training Instructor at Mychett, joined the Company towards the end of the month. He was already a household name in Rugby League circles, as his son Bev was to be after the war. The sterling work done by Jock Gray during the formation and training of the Company was recognised when he was granted an emergency commission as a Second Lieutenant with the Company. As the CMP did not have its own Corps of Officers at this time he reverted to his former Regiment, The Kings. Sergeant G.D.Thomas was promoted to replace him as RSM.

At the end of June the Company vacated their garage in Mascara and headed east for Sousse in preparation for the invasion of Sicily. A train party left with the Company's baggage on the 29th, with the main body travelling the 600 miles by road the following day. The rail journey appears to have been by far the more memorable, as described by Roy Tyler:

> *The train was named 'The Eastern Belle' and consisted of cattle trucks, each labelled 40 MEN or 8 HORSES, and two old Third Class wooden coaches for the Officers. As a Troop Train it had its failings. One thing was that only the fleetest of men could get tea, for the engine driver would only let so many tap his boiler. The remainder had to do without. Washing facilities did not exist, and toilets were wherever the train stopped, which it often did. This was a very dodgy operation because invariably the train started off at the most inappropriate of times. Massed soldiery would rise from all over the countryside, grasping trousers in one hand and frantically waving with the other. Occasionally one would wave with both hands with consequent loss of dignity. It was*

little short of a miracle that we only left three men behind during the journey. Sadly, we lost another who fell under the wheels of the train and was cut in half. The OC Train, a young Captain from the Parachute Regiment, stopped perambulating up and down the train warning everyone of the dire consequences of selling kit to the locals, only to discover that each time he returned his own kit was that little bit less.

Scattered all over the mountains were little farms, worked only by women, occasionally one saw a man busily thinking on his back under a tree. These hardy Berber girls all dressed alike in long red night-dress like garments and nothing else. Should the train chug slowly by, or as was more often the case, halt near one, she would lift her skirt to cover her face from the contaminating gaze of we unbelievers! But there it was – a most peculiar custom. You can bet your bottom dollar that if you meet a man of my vintage who cannot look a woman in the face he once travelled on 'The Eastern Belle'.

At Sousse the Company was camped in olive groves close to the village of M'Saken, and next to a camp holding 'Popski's Private Army'. Vladimir Peniakof, or Popski was a Belgian of Russian parentage who commanded a small independent raiding unit. He and his men were frequent visitors to the Military Police lines and there soon developed a mutual respect between the two units. In due course a boxing match was arranged, over a few glasses of the local brew no doubt, but the invasion of Italy caused it to be cancelled, much to the relief of the CMP 'volunteers'.

To bring the Company up to strength more volunteers were recruited from other CMP units serving in the Middle East. Parachute training for them was completed as and when the opportunity arose. A number of volunteers came from the 6th Armoured Division Provost Company and completed their jumps at Kairouan Airfield near Sousse, for one of them with near fatal consequences. Lance Corporal Harold Bennett landed heavily on his entrenching tool on one jump which gave him a severe 'sitting down' problem for a few days. On his next jump he became entangled in his own parachute rigging lines and received severe burns. Undaunted he carried on to complete the course and to distinguish himself later at Arnhem.

As was normal custom and practice with a CMP unit, when other troops were on 'Stand-Down' after a day's training, or were enjoying a spell of recreation, the Military Policeman had his Police Duties to perform. Traffic Control, Security Duties, Town Patrols and Patrols of the local Out of Bounds areas. Roy Tyler recalls one particular road junction heavily used by military traffic:

An important 'T' junction stands in the middle of M'Saken, one road leading off to Sfax, one to Kairouan and the third to Enfidaville. In the angle of the junction is a raised cemetery, prominent in which was a shell damaged tomb with the occupant visible to all. He rapidly became known as 'Old Charlie' and many military drivers were told to 'Turn Left' or 'Right' at 'Old Charlie' then 'Keep straight on'. 'Old Charlie' became known throughout the Division.
This was good experience in utilising local resources for Traffic Control. Sleep well Charlie, you did a good job and, unlike Discs Directional, no Arab ever wanted to pinch you.

Early in July the Company was paraded and all those with previous infantry experience, some twenty-one Senior and Junior Ranks, were placed on stand-by for the imminent invasion of Sicily. The Division's role in the invasion has been fully documented elsewhere, but a brief outline of its objectives is necessary to understand the part played by the Military Police.

With enemy resistance in Tunisia at an end, the British 8th Army, together with the US 7th Army began its invasion of Sicily on the 10th of July. From the invasion beaches in the south of the island the Allies were to race up the coast road to the east of Mount Etna and capture the port of Messina prior to striking out for the Italian mainland. The 1st Airlanding Brigade and the 1st Parachute Brigade were to launch two separate operations, each having as their objectives bridges over which the coast road passed. That the two airborne operations did not become total disasters is due almost entirely to the training, courage and determination of the paratroopers taking part.

The airborne operations had a less than auspicious start as the Airlanding Brigade took off in their unfamiliar, overloaded WACO gliders from the crude desert airstrips into excessively strong winds. The gliders were towed by a mixture of Dakotas, Halifaxes and Albemarles, many piloted by raw US pilots who had little or no experience of towing gliders. Although the plan called for the pilots to release their gliders before reaching the coast of Sicily, many were released too far out at sea with little chance of reaching land, and with disastrous consequences for the heavily laden passengers. Many other gliders were severely damaged or shot out of the sky by trigger-happy gunners on Allied ships heading for the invasion beaches. Of the 148 gliders which lifted off from North Africa carrying the 2000 men of the Airlanding Brigade, 2 suffered broken tow ropes on take off, 5 did not cross the North African coast, 4 returned to base behind their tow aircraft, 69 landed in the sea, 59 actually landed in Sicily but were scattered over an area of 25 square miles, and 9 were unaccounted for at the end of the day. Only 12 gliders landed on the assigned Landing Zones. The Airlanding Brigade lost almost 500 men of the original 2,000, and 88 highly trained Glider Pilots.

The 3 Battalions of the 1st Parachute Brigade followed four days later on the 13th July and suffered similar misfortune. Flying in US piloted Dakotas, the 1900 paratroopers of the Brigade were subjected to poor navigation and further anti-aircraft fire from the tense sailors manning the guns on the Allied invasion ships. Close to the target enemy flak alarmed the inexperienced pilots who took drastic evasive action and consequently became so disoriented that the paratroopers were dropped over a widely scattered area, often many miles from the planned Dropping Zone. Of the 1900 all ranks who left North Africa, less than 300 were available to capture the Brigade's objectives. Almost 30% of the total were landed back in North Africa without having fired a shot in anger.

Into this maelstrom were pitched the twenty-one 'infantry experienced' Military Policemen. Their part in the Operation is vividly told in the reports submitted to their Officer Commanding immediately they returned to Company HQ in Sousse.

Corporals Fielding and Formoy, together with Lance Corporals Cox and Dale, were attached to the Airlanding Brigade which was

Map 1
North Africa and Sicily Operations

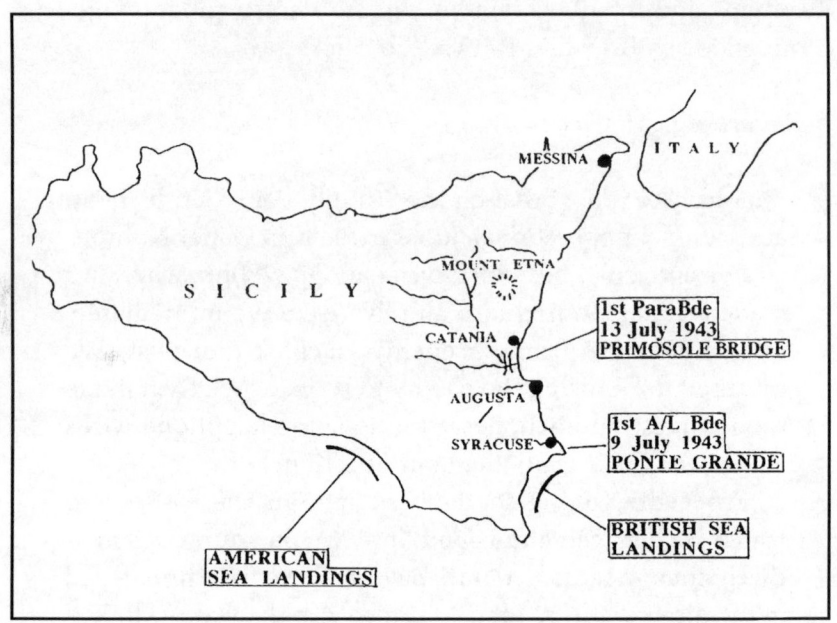

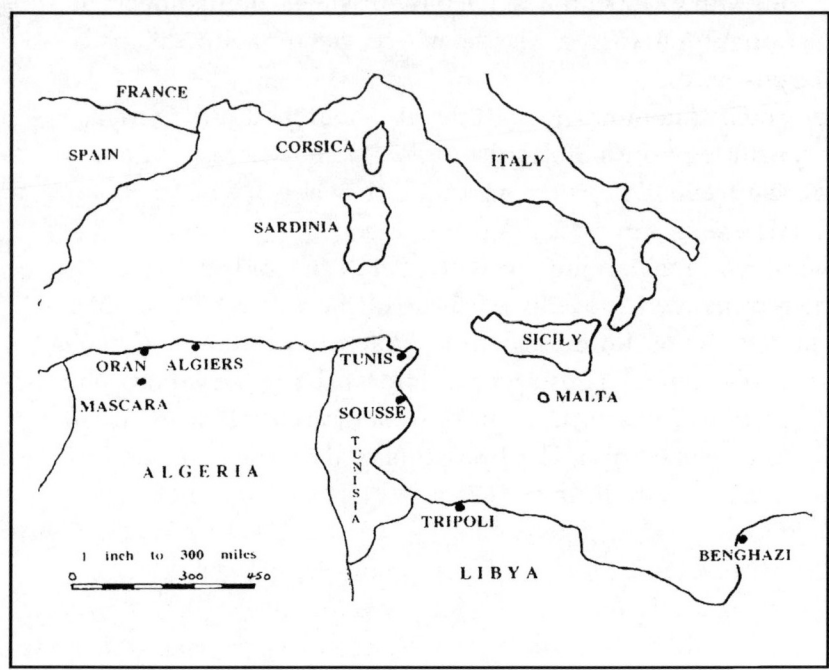

tasked with capturing and holding the Ponte Grande Road Bridge south of Syracuse, and the port of Syracuse itself. The Brigade comprised the 1st and 2nd battalions of the South Staffordshire Regiment and 1st Battalion of the Border Regiment and was commanded by Brigadier P.H.W. 'Pip' Hicks.

Report of Lcpl. Cox:

Sir, I have to report that on the 9th July 1943 I left 'B' Strip at 1840hrs for operational duties in Sicily in Glider Number 34. We arrived at our objective at about 2230hrs where we made a crash landing into an olive tree. We immediately came under fire from an enemy machine gun post. We returned fire causing the enemy to retreat. We then made for a narrow lane where we found some telephone wires which we cut, putting them out of action.

Proceeding along the lane we met an enemy Section which we engaged and wiped out. We dug ourselves in at this point and remained until daybreak when we proceeded in the direction of 'Waterloo Bridge'. On the way we linked up with Colonel Jones, (Deputy Brigade Commander) and proceeded to the bridge where we took up defensive positions.

On the morning of 10th July I marched into Syracuse with the South Staffordshire Regiment where I remained until about 2000hrs on the 13th when I embarked for Sousse.

On the 12th July the AB64 Part 1 of Cpl Formoy, CMP, was handed to me by a Private of the South Staffordshire Regiment who informed me that Cpl Formoy had been badly injured in a glider crash and had been carried to safety in a small vineyard. On making enquiries from the men who had been in this glider I was informed that Cpl Formoy had been taken to hospital.

Lcpl M. Cox
In the Field
15 July 1943

Report of Lcpl Dale:

Sir, I have to report that on the 9th July 1943 I was instructed to report to the Border Regiment for Police Duties on 'Scheme Horrific'. I was briefed by the Adjutant of the Regiment who explained that the destination was to be Sicily and that I would travel in one of the Rifle Company gliders and then join HQ Company on reaching the destination.

I was attached to Number 9 Platoon of 'A' Company who were allotted glider Number 103. We left Number 3 strip at Airfield 'D' about 1915hrs on the 9th July.

In company with many other aircraft we headed towards our objective at almost sea level, (approx 200 feet). The sea crossing to within sight of our objective was uneventful except for a glimpse of the seaborne invasion fleet soon after sunset. Soon after sighting land at approx 2200hrs our glider cast off from the tug 'plane. This seemed a bit strange to me as, according to our briefing, we were to release at 1100 feet, 3000 yards from land, yet it was obvious that our height was less and the distance to shore considerably more. I though about three to five miles.

I had no sooner checked my equipment when the Senior Glider Pilot, a Staff Sergeant of the Army Air Corps, told us that we would be landing in the sea and that we were to discard our equipment and open all the doors. The glider landed in the sea fairly smoothly and we had ample time to escape from the cabin before it filled with water. On checking up on personnel whilst sitting on the wings one Lance Corporal from the Border Regiment was found to be missing.

For a while the sea was very calm, but later a heavy swell came from the direction of the land and after about two hours the machine broke up, both wings and the tail coming adrift. To ease the weight on the waterlogged machine for non-swimmers, myself and another man, (name unknown to me), attempted to swim to the beach. After about half an hour, and due to heavy seas, I lost contact with my companion and continued swimming towards the faint outline of the coast. My last recollection was of seeing the sun above the horizon. I then found myself wrapped in blankets on board an invasion barge and the crew informed me that I had been picked out of the water at about 0730hrs. After landing the troops on the beach the barge returned to its Base Ship, SS DEVONSHIRE, where I was left in the care of the Medical Staff.

The DEVONSHIRE proceeded to Suez where, together with survivors of the Division, I spent two days in the Transit Camp. I spent a further 14 days in the 2nd I.T.D.Camp Genifia, before returning via Benghazi to Company lines at 1800hrs on the 1st of August.

Lcpl P. Dale
In the Field
2 August 1943

Peter Dale was not alone in having to discard his equipment and start swimming for the shore. Brigadier Hicks and his own personal Glider Pilot, none other than Colonel Chatterton, Commanding Officer of the Glider Pilot Regiment, also came down in the sea and had to swim to shore. Lcpl Dale was to distinguish himself further the following year during the Division's evacuation from Oosterbeek.

At 4pm on the 13th of July a further 17 NCOs left Company HQ on attachment to the Battalions of the 1st Parachute Brigade for Operation Fustian, the airborne landings on Sicily. The Brigade's objective was the steel girder bridge spanning the River Simeto at Primosole south of Catania.

Report of Sgt Callaway:

Sir, I have to report that on the 11th July 1943, Cpl Strand, Lcpls Watson, Buttery, James, Barlow and myself were attached to the 3rd Parachute Battalion for operations. We were briefed on the whole operation and our role as Military Policemen. We were dropped on the night of 13th July. The plane was caught in searchlights and there was also very heavy anti-aircraft fire. Whilst jumping, tracer bullets came at us from all directions.

On reaching the ground it was obvious that we had been dropped on the wrong DZ and were in the middle of a well defended enemy location. I realised that my role as a Military Policeman was finished and I therefore adopted that of a parachutist. On the DZ I made my way to where the containers should have been, and I picked up my NCOs. We crossed a river and on the other side I made contact with 7 paratroopers from the 3rd Battalion. There was no sign of Lt. Mansfield or the Section Sergeant. Fires were burning all around us and machine gun fire and shots were coming from all directions. Several screams were heard coming from the direction of the fires.

We saw a C47 Dakota caught in heavy anti-aircraft fire, burst in to flames and lose height rapidly. Two parachutes opened and appeared to come down with the plane. Realising that there was nothing we could do at that time I made a mental note of the location of the plane for future identification. We continued to make our way across country until we came to a large shell hole. We had no sooner taken cover when we saw a plane and glider crash in the distance. I asked for three volunteers for a Patrol to get the lay of the ground and also to do anything possible for the occupants of the plane and glider. The Patrol consisted of Lcpls Buttery and Watson and Private Easton of the Parachute Regiment. I told them that the rest of us would remain in our present position until the moon went down.

Later we heard shots coming from the direction the Patrol had taken and, after waiting until the agreed time, we moved our position. We made for the river, found cover, and rested for the day. Later one of the sentries pointed out to me a German patrol with two Airborne prisoners. I also saw TCVs carrying German infantry, also tanks, presumably Herman Goering P IVs, advancing east along the road approximately 200 yards to our front.

Later we tried without success to make our way to the bridge which was the original objective. After a further two days of hiding we decided to split in to small groups and attempt to make our way back to Allied lines, doing whatever damage we could wherever possible. We left at intervals in twos and threes. I was with Privates Stansbury and Smallman of the Parachute Regiment.

Time elapsed and we were getting very tired and hungry. We came to a farmhouse and decided to attack it as our hunger was getting the better of us. We rushed the farmhouse but were amazed to find six Sicilians inside who welcomed us with open arms. There we ate and slept in rotation. During this time planes were passing overhead and bombing about 600 yards west of the farm. We learnt from the Sicilians that it was an Italian airfield.

We left that night and made for the airfield to do whatever damage we could. We fired two planes and then got out as quickly as possible. We met no opposition but made it a very short stay as we had seen German patrols in the vicinity during the day.

For two days we carried on hiding, crawling and infiltrating. We came across a crashed and burnt out aircraft which appeared similar to a C47. All the occupants were burnt beyond recognition. We could not get any identity discs off the bodies as it would have meant digging in the debris and shifting the whole lot which was unsafe as we were not far from the main road. We found a body which appeared to be that of the pilot approximately 20 yards from the plane. The only identification we could find of the aircraft was a small container with six black stripes and the number '12' on it. I would estimate that there were about 10 bodies in the wreckage.

The following day we met up with a unit of the 8th Army to whom I gave all the information we had gathered. After resting and eating we were taken to Syracuse and from there to Malta where we were re-clothed and taken by ship to Suez.

Sgt H. Callaway
In the Field
27 July 1943

Of the five NCOs of the Company who went to Sicily with Sgt 'Cab' Calloway only two found their way back to Sousse. Strand, Barlow and Buttery were captured and spent the remainder of the war as prisoners. Sgt. Calloway went on to lead his section to capture the Arnhem Police Station the following September.

Report of Lcpl Watson:

Sir, I have to report that on the 13th July 1943 I was attached to 'C' Company of the 3rd Parachute Battalion. We emplaned at 'B' Strip at 1930hrs and took off at 2000hrs. Cpl Strand and Lcpl Barlow were in aircraft Number 86, and Sgt Callaway, Lcpls James, Buttery and myself were in Number 87. The flight to the Sicilian coast was uneventful.

As we approached the coast we received the order to hitch our static lines and about the same time Ack-Ack shells burst around the aircraft rocking it considerably. We remained standing ready to jump and the plane flew down to ground level. We flew low for about twenty minutes then the plane climbed to about 500 feet and we had the Red Light followed quickly by the Green. Everybody left the plane immediately, this would be about 2310hrs, and we were machine gunned all the way down.

Some five minutes after landing I saw a Douglas aircraft coming down in flames about a mile away. I also saw at least three parachutes come from it and open.

I contacted Sgt Callaway and Lcpls James and Buttery. We tried to pinpoint our exact position but were unable to do so as we were not on the DZ. We tried to locate the rest of the stick and found them all with the exception of Lt. Mansfield and three men. Sgt. Callaway took charge and we moved across country for about two hours before resting in a large bomb crater.

Whilst resting we saw in the distance a plane hit the ground and burst in to flames. A glider was seen to skim the top of the burning plane. We were expecting gliders to arrive with 6 Pounder guns, so Lcpl Buttery, Private Easton of 'C' Company and myself set off to try and either salvage the gun or contact any of the crew. On arriving at the spot where the plane was still burning we found that the glider had also burnt out. It was impossible to recognise the type of plane or glider. None of the personnel could be found alive. Nearby was a building with two lorries parked in a field. One lorry had a triangle of light shining upwards from the cab.

The three of us set off to return to Sgt. Callaway, but Lcpl Buttery said he was staying as it was a good position to hold. Private Easton and I left telling Buttery that we would bring the rest of the party to him. We marched for about two hours during which time the moon went down and we became lost. We took cover in a ditch and rested until it was light enough to see. We saw the river in the distance and, as it offered the only cover on the plain, we set off for it. We reached the river and worked our way along the bank keeping to cover and resting at regular intervals. About 0900hrs we contacted Major Bush of 'C' Company and about a dozen men who were lying up in the tall grass.

We remained with this party and lay up for most of the day, moving again at night. With stragglers the party became about 35 strong. We took 15 prisoners.

About 0100hrs on the 16th July we linked up with advance units of the 8th Army and spent the night at Lentini. About 1800hrs the following day we marched about 2 miles down the road to Augusta and from there obtained transport to Syracuse. There we embarked on a Tank Transporter ship to return to North Africa. We sailed on the 17th. After breakfast at 3rd Battalion lines in Sousse I returned to my own unit HQ.

Lcpl D. Watson
In the Field
26 July 1943

Like a true policeman Lance Corporal Watson got his priorities in order. He made sure he had his breakfast first before reporting back to CMP Company HQ.

Report of Lcpl Pummell:

Sir, I have to report that at 'F' strip on Tuesday 13th July 1943 I was Number 1 in aircraft Number 1130 attached to 1st Parachute Brigade HQ. Lcpls Evans and Page were Numbers 2 and 3 and Sgt Whitehead Number 4 as Stickmaster.

We took off about 2115hrs and about 2300hrs, whilst flying over the sea were fired on by a ship. I was sitting in the tail of the aircraft and, looking down, could see a vessel. It looked like a small merchant ship, but I was unable to identify its nationality. Shortly afterwards I saw the coast of Sicily approaching and we met very heavy anti-aircraft fire.

We jumped at about 2340hrs. Fire from the ground was pretty heavy and I noticed that it came from some hills to my left. I landed safely on the correct DZ and about 30 yards from the RV which was a small farmhouse. I made my way to the RV and shortly afterwards Sgt Whitehead and Lcpl Evans arrived with four other men out of our stick. Lcpl Page was not to be seen.

The farmhouse came under heavy shell fire and we were told to form up ready to move. There were about 15 men in our party and as we approached a small bridge where the road crossed a dried up stream we met some more of Brigade HQ personnel, including the Brigade Commander. It was now the early hours of the 14th July and we made our way to the bridge across the River Simeto. We reached the bridge despite an enemy searchlight which kept us constantly going to ground. On reaching the bridge we found that it was already in our possession and there was a large number of personnel from different units on the road and around the bridge. In the darkness, and owing to the large number of men in the vicinity, I lost contact with the party I had arrived with. I did not see Sgt Whitehead or Lcpl Evans again. I stayed at the bridge until daylight, during which time we came under small arms fire. On the north side of the bridge an enemy ammunition convoy was intercepted and destroyed, the flames lighting up the bridge. At daylight I crossed to the north side of the bridge and endeavoured to contact Sgt Whitehead and the section to which I was attached. I could not locate them.

I then attached myself to 'S' Company of the 1st Parachute Battalion. I had a rifle and ammunition which had been unclaimed at the original RV. After about 4 hours we were ordered to 'Stand By' as an enemy patrol with an armoured car was approaching our position. The enemy was engaged by our mortar. Some time later we were attacked and machine gunned from the air, after which enemy ground forces opened fire on us with small arms, mortars and what I took to be light Artillery. We returned fire with rifle and Bren. This continued throughout the day and the fire from the enemy indicated that we were out numbered.

At about 1730hrs I saw the enemy approaching across the fields which were covered with small bushes. We opened fire, but were ordered to retire. I was told to follow a party which was moving out whilst some of the men formed a rearguard. We crossed the fields and came under heavy small arms fire.

On reaching the river we crossed and took cover in a large fold in the ground. Some of the men were detailed to line the river bank and stop the enemy from crossing. When darkness came we split up in to small parties and were told that we were to make our way to the coast.

After we had marched for some time we came to an orange grove where we met some more of the Brigade. We slept until morning. On continuing our march the following day we came to a large plain from where we could see the sea. We could hear artillery fire close by and some of our Officers patrolled the area and contacted units of the British Forces. We continued on to Syracuse from where transport was arranged to return us to Sousse.

Lcpl J. Pummell
In the Field
26 July 1943

Of the original party of 4 Military Policemen, Pummell and Evans succeeded in getting back to Sousse. Sgt Whitehead and Lcpl Monty Page were captured. They were to meet up in POW Camp with other members of the company captured at Arnhem.

The final report is from the group who were attached to 2nd Battalion of the Parachute Regiment. Their experience was also shared by many other groups of the Brigade who found themselves in small groups deep in enemy held territory, and many miles from the designated DZ.

Report of Lcpl Teece:

Sir, I have to report that on Monday 12th July 1943 I was attached to 'B' Company, 2nd Battalion of the Parachute Regiment, together with Lcpls Inns and Stubbs, CMP.

We emplaned at approx. 1915hrs and jumped at about 2240hrs. On landing we discovered that we had been dropped about 20 miles North West of the correct DZ.

We searched and located the rest of the Section with the exception of three men. We then came under the orders of Captain Crawley, who was 2i/c of 'B' Company, 2nd Battalion. The same night we marched through the hours of darkness for about 10 hours in a due south direction. During the hours of daylight we hid in bamboo canes.

At approx. 2030hrs on the 14th July we were preparing to move off when the sentry reported that parachute troops were being dropped about ¾ of a mile away from aircraft identified as enemy. Captain Crawley decided that we would remain overnight where we were. We remained there until approx. 2100hrs on the 15th and then moved off again. That night we met no enemy opposition, but had to cross the River Simeto. During the day of the 16th we lay up on the banks of a stream which was about 50 yards north of the raised road known as 'CATERPILLAR'. We resumed our march about 2130hrs and whilst crossing the raised road we came under fire from one or two snipers. At approx. 0400hrs on the 17th we made contact with the advanced Mobile Tank Unit of the 50th Division, 8th Army.

During the time we were behind enemy lines we never met any of the other airborne troops.

Lcpl P. Teece
In the Field
27 July 1943

Sir, We have read over and corroborate the above report.

Lcpl R. Inns
Lcpl H. Stubbs

Bill Inns had achieved a number of 'firsts' on this operation. It was his first night jump, his first from a Dakota, his first taste of action and the first time he had jumped with a rifle strapped to his leg. He remembers:

As we flew in there was a lot of flak coming up. The Dispatcher started screaming "Get out! Get out!" So we went. We were very low and I hit the deck with such a thump, right on my backside. I was dazed for quite a while afterwards. We formed up, checked the map, and realised we had been dropped miles away from the DZ. When I came to use my rifle it was clogged with earth half way up the barrel where it had dug in when I landed. At one point we climbed to the top of a mountain and the guns were firing over the top. We could actually see the shells passing overhead.

Of the twenty-one Provost NCOs who took part in the invasion, 9 were captured and 12 eventually made their way back to Company HQ in Sousse. There was a great feeling of loss and sadness for the 9 members of the close-knit Company who failed to return, and it was to be some months before it was learnt that they were alive and being held prisoner.

In the meantime, parachute training continued for the recent arrivals. A section was detached for duty at the Hammam Lif Rest Camp and, as was the case with the rest of the Division, the remainder of the Company spent 48 hours leave there in rotation. Joe Smith was a sergeant with the 21st Independent Parachute Company at the time and had served pre-war in the Territorial Army with John Hamblett and Dennis Riley. He met them again in North Africa when he was spending a few days at the Rest Camp after the Sicily invasion.

> *I took advantage of the Passion Wagon to sample the flesh pots of Tunis. After a miserable pint of 'Cat's P' at the huge Naafi, and wandering along a truly French boulevard overrun with service types of all shapes, nationalities, colours and sizes, I ran in to John Hamblett on Patrol. At 6 foot 3 inches I could hardly miss him. Explaining my circumstances to him I was promptly taken in charge and deposited in the local Provost Mess with instructions to the Barman to keep my glass replenished with Worthington whenever the need arose. After a splendid lunch I accompanied John on Patrol which included a tour of the Out of Bounds areas which inevitably included one of the establishments catering for the varying needs of the male at large and on the loose. In retrospect it was all rather dull and unexciting, and the price of the booze was exorbitant but, and this I can remember with startling clarity, it was peaceful, cool and quiet. Tantamount to a miracle in North Africa in the high summer of 1943.*

It was at this time that the Company Commander Captain K.G. Wells, was admitted to the local Military hospital and relinquished command. His place was taken by Lieutenant P.B. Thomas of the Royal Artillery who was promoted to Captain.

Early in September 1943, 16 man Sections under Lieutenants Clarke and Risman were attached to the 4th and 2nd Parachute Brigades respectively in preparation for the Division's move to Italy. Sadly on the eve of departure, Lance Corporal Robert Lamb was fatally injured when the motor cycle he was riding pillion on ran in to an Arab cart in the dark. The 35 year old came from Liverpool and is now laid to rest in the Enfidaville Cemetery in Tunis. The motor cycle rider Lance Corporal 'Canada' Young was uninjured.

Following the surrender of Italy and the signing of an Armistice on the 3rd of September, 1st Airborne Division was ordered to occupy the port of Taranto, in the heel of Italy, and to hold it until the arrival of reinforcements. Between the 8th and 12th of September 3 Officers and 62 NCOs from the Provost Company embarked at Bizerta in Tunisia aboard various Royal Navy ships, including HMS Aurora, HMS Dido and HMS Penelope, and landed at Taranto. The Division met only light opposition and the port was soon in Allied hands. Two Provost Sections remained behind in Sousse as Rear Party to protect the Division's reserve of stores and equipment from being pilfered by local 'souvenir hunters'.

The advance northwards from Taranto began immediately against strong opposition from German Parachute troops and it was whilst observing an attack by the British 10th Parachute Battalion that the Divisional Commander, Major General Hopkinson, was mortally wounded by enemy machine gun fire. At the funeral on the 14th September members of the Provost Company proudly carried their Commander's coffin to its final resting place.

The Company were soon donning Duty Order of the familiar SD caps with red cap covers and settling in to the role of Military Policemen again. Having left the unit transport in North Africa it was necessary to obtain vehicles and motor cycles and these were quickly commandeered from the defeated Italian Army and Carabiniere. German Army stragglers were rounded up and placed under close guard. Foot and Mobile patrols of the town commenced and Security Duties at Div. HQ. This was situated in the Albergo Europa which had been hastily vacated by the Germans as the British landed.

As a seaport, Taranto was not alone in having a Red Light area with seedy bars and even seedier brothels. The latter were immediately placed 'Out of Bounds' by the Military Authorities, and it fell to the likes of Jock Moir, 'Junior' Stubbs, Harold Mason and the other Junior NCOs to try and implement these Military Instructions. A thankless task in any part of the world when the licentious soldiery are out for a night on the town, but even more difficult when those soldiers are Airborne and the Military Policemen are outnumbered by around 100 to 1!!

Provost Sections were constantly on the move with brief attachments to either the Airlanding Brigade or to one of the Parachute Brigades for a specific task. It was essential for the Sections to be completely self-contained, both in vehicles and in equipment as a short notice move with one of the Brigades could take them many miles from Company HQ. Traffic Control and Escort Duties were yet another Provost task as units were moved to and from the forward battle areas. A thorough test of the NCO's driving and riding skills, his proficiency at map reading and his ability to take control at a busy road junction, often under attack from enemy artillery or aircraft.

By mid-September the Airborne Division had advanced some 40 miles up the east coast and by the 17th had occupied the airfield at Gioia as the German Army hastily withdrew northwards. The Provost Company advanced with the Division and settled in to accommodation at Gioia at the end of the month. Throughout October the pattern was much the same as the previous month with groups of NCOs being detached for a few days at a time to one of the Brigades located up and down that stretch of coastline. Harold Mason and 'Junior' Stubbs were young Lance Corporals with Sergeant Austin Roberts' Section and spent some time in the costal town of Barletta practising landings from Infantry Landing Craft in preparation for the possible seaborne landing further north.

As more units of the 8th Army arrived in Italy the 1st Airborne Division was withdrawn from the line and returned to Taranto to sail for England in preparation for the invasion of Europe. They left behind the 2nd Parachute Brigade to act in an independent capacity. Volunteers were required from the Div. Provost Company to remain in Italy and form the new 2nd Independent Parachute Brigade Provost Section. Sgt Vic Woods had recently been commissioned and commanded the Section which was made up of 21, mainly single NCOs and volunteers. They left to join the new Brigade on the 22nd November 1943. Within a month Lieutenant Woods and two of his men, Lance Corporals McBride and Cooke, were killed when their vehicle received a direct hit from an enemy shell. Lance Corporals 'Tosh' Richards and 'Dodger' Trickett were escorting a battalion of New Zealand troops in to the line when they came across the wrecked Jeep by the side of the road. The badly wounded

Policemen had been carried in to a nearby house, but there was little that Richards and Trickett could do but get their comrades to a Forward Aid Post as quickly as possible. By the morning all three had died. They are buried together at the Sangro River War Cemetery in Italy.

As 1943 drew to a close the Company left Italy and sailed for England with the rest of the Division. Meanwhile, the two Sections left behind as Rear Party in Sousse undertook a lengthy 500 mile rail journey back across the Atlas Mountains to a temporary stay in a tented transit camp at Blida outside Algiers, before they too were to return to England. Roy Tyler remembers his Christmas Dinner in the tented camp as..."Biscuits, corned beef and sardines washed down with a shared can of beer, and the rain falling in torrents as we listened to a crackling radio bringing the King's Christmas Speech from home".... Of this wartime memories are made.

Training Wing Instructors, CMP Depot, Mytchett, March 1942 Rear row extreme left Sgt. A. McKnight. Middle row extreme left. Sgt. W. Kibble Front row fourth from right CSM W.B. Gray

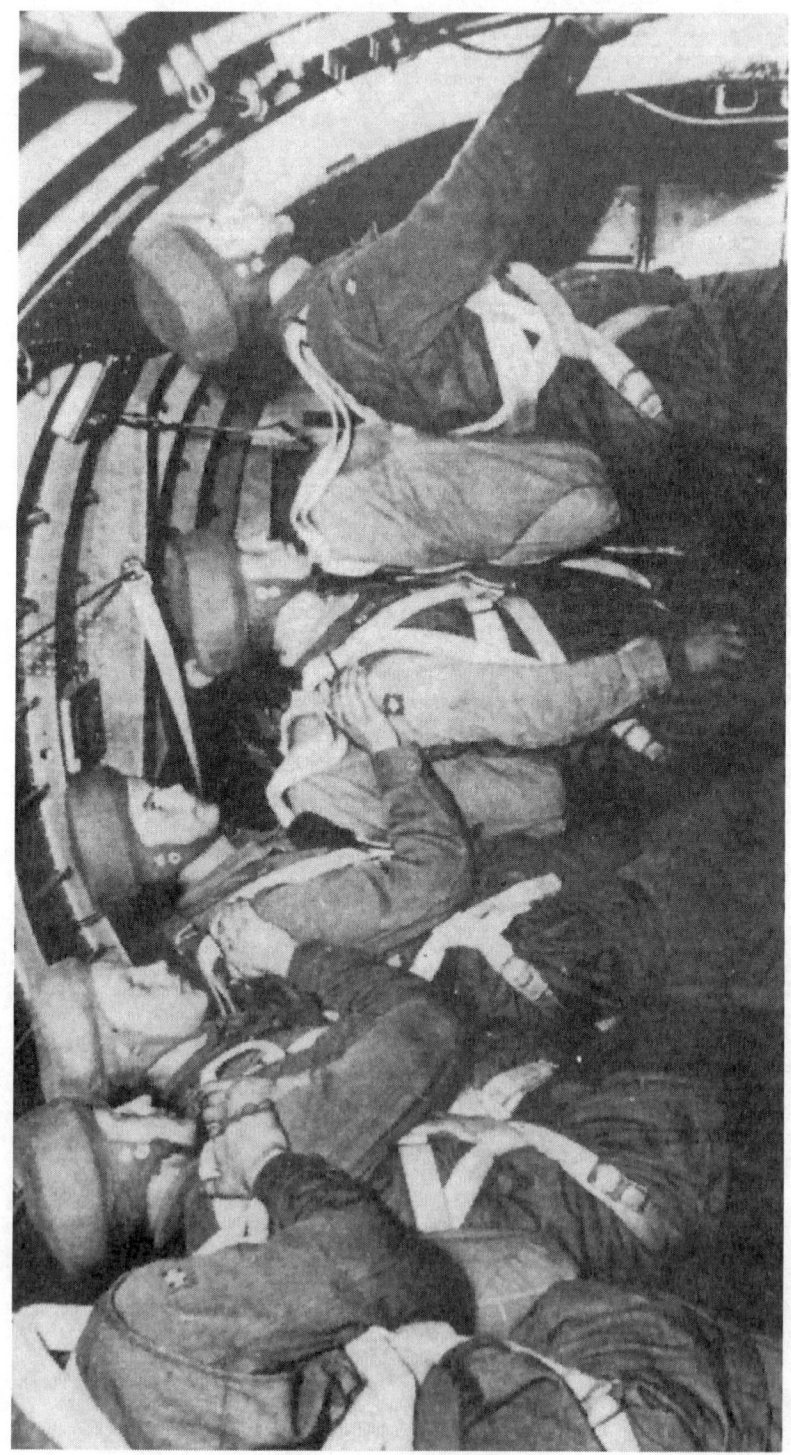

Training at Ringway - Exit from a Dakota for these recruits

No. 1 Section (att 1 Para Bde) May/June 1944 at Stubton. L/R rear Lcpls H.Day, O. Wright, J. McGaw, J. Coates, J. Plummell, J. Keddie, F. Wilkinson, A. Rodgers. L/R front Lcpls K. Glover, R. North, Cpl H. Bennett, Sgt H. 'Cab' Callaway, Lt W. Morley, Cpl J. Peers, Lcpl M. Cox.

No. 2 Section (att 4 Para Bde) May/June 1944 at Stubton. L/R rear Lcpl W. Bazeley, T. Teece, P. Coppinger, F. Cardinelli, J. Ford, J. Harris, H. Stubbs, J. Raine. L/R centre Cpl J. Mills, Sgt A. Roberts, Lt F de R Locke, Major O.P. Haig, Capt W. Gray, Cpl L. Formoy, Lcpl H. Wiffen. L/R front W. Inns and mascot, C. Baker, J. Killen, J Lawton.

North Africa, Sicily and Italy

No. 3 Section (att Airlanding Bde) May/June 1944 at Stubton. L/R rear Lcpls D. Fitzgerald, H. Glennon, J. Pawsey, T. Mason, H. Charles, J. Howells, B. O'Quinn, D. Riley. L/R front Lcpl E. Miller, Cpl J. Moir, Sgt N. Phillips, Capt W. Gray, Lt F. Horton, Cpl R. Fielding, Lcpl H. Williams.

No. 4 Section (att Div. HQ) May/June 1944 at Stubton. L/R rear Lcpls P. Jones, J. Evans, J. Unsworth, A. Hackett, H. Wilce, J. Haycock. L/R centre Lcpl E. Hookway, Cpl F. Hodgson, Capt B. Gray, Major O.P. Haig Lt R Falck, Sgt D. Yardley, Cpl P. Dale. L/R front Lcpls J. Newby, A. Storry, W. Millar, S. Reast, J. Mole.

Reinforcement Section (Mainly Rear Party and Seaborne Elements) May/June 1944 at Stubton. L/R rear Lcpls R. Ogilvie, A. Fitzpatrick, E. Robinson, A. Thelwall, W. MacIntosh, D. Wilkins, R. Burrows, G. Reah. L/R front Lcpls R. Tittensor, W. Nugent, T. Pentney, Lt W. Morley, Sgt R. 'Mac' McKnight, Cpl J. Peers, Lcpl J. Griggs.

HQ Section (att Div. HQ) May/June 1944 at Stubton. L/R rear Lcpls B. Croft, L. Sarbutt, K. 'Canada' Young, Cpl H. Levy, Lcpls S. Chaplin, H. Nunn, J. Hall, J. Langton. L/R centre W. Hinchliffe, Cpl R. England, Sgt E. Howard, Capt B. Gray, CQMS R. Pell, Sgt D. Barnett, Cpl J. Hamblett. L/R front Lcpls J. Gommersall, G. Perrot, J. Tofield, Cpl A. Armstrong, Lcpls L. Clarke, E. Clements.

CHAPTER 3

A LINCOLNSHIRE INTERVAL

*The RSM entered the Nissen Hut and fired off a few
rounds from his Sten*

(John Hamblett)

The main body of the Company docked at Liverpool on the 10th December 1943 after an uneventful passage home from Italy. Home to a chilly December morning, and an even chillier reception from the over-zealous Customs and Excise Officials. Wartime austerity in England meant a drastic shortage of the two comforts which the average soldier holds dear – cigarettes and beer. But it was great to be home again.

The Division was to be based around the Lincolnshire countryside with the Provost Company billeted at Stubton Hall in the quiet little village of Stubton. The cluster of neat houses and farms was just off the main A1 road between Newark and Grantham and was to be the home for the Company HQ for the next 9 months. The NCOs were immediately sent on 14 days well deserved Disembarkation Leave and returned to Stubton just in time to see the Rear Party arrive from North Africa and disappear on leave also.

Stubton Hall was a small family residence built in the Georgian style and standing in its own grounds. The Hall had been requisitioned by the War Office and a number of Nissen huts erected in the grounds to serve as billets, dining hall, stores etc. The Company Officers lived in part of the Hall along with the owner and his family. Close by was the village Rectory which was the temporary wartime home of a bevy of attractive Land Army girls, much to the delight and surprise of the young Military Policemen. It wasn't long before dances, record evenings and other social activities were organised between the two groups. At one such gathering, soon after the Company had arrived at Stubton, Harry Wilce watched spell-bound as some of the Land Army lasses downed their beer out of a pint pot. To someone who had not seen real beer for a very long time, nor an English woman come to that, this was truly an amazing sight. One young lady was quickly giving the nickname 'Half-Pint' by the NCOs, more in recognition of her height than her drinking prowess. Many amorous liaisons were formed during those months at Stubton, some short but sweet, some to founder when he failed to return from Arnhem, others like Harry and Hilda Wilce cemented their relationship with wedding bells and are still happily married to this day. (We managed to trace 'Half-Pint' only a month before this book went to the printers. She had married Lcpl Jock Wright who was captured at the Arnhem Police Station, survived Prison Camp, but sadly passed away in 1993.)

January 1944 was a settling in period as the Company prepared, along with the rest of the Division for the prospect of an Allied invasion of Europe. Those NCOs lost in Sicily and to the Second Independent Parachute Brigade had to be replaced and their places were filled by the likes of Jack Coates, Dennis Fitzgerald, John 'Claude' Raine and Charles 'Yoxy' Baker, all of whom transferred to the CMP from the Parachute Regiment. In all, no fewer than 27 reinforcements joined the Company from training at the Mytchett Depot. The Company had also to replace equipment left behind in North Africa, with the first priority being transport, and during the month they took delivery of a number of 15cwt trucks, 8 motorcycle combinations and 54 solo machines.

Dozens of towns and villages around the Lincolnshire and Leicestershire were suddenly occupied by men wearing the Red Beret. Large country halls and mansions, stables, empty houses, farm buildings, all were requisitioned to house the thousands of troops. The good folk of Grantham, Spalding, Bourne, Woodall Spa, Melton Mowbray and the close knit communities of Claypole, Barkeston, and Stapleford Park faced the 'invasion' with a certain amount of trepidation. But their fears were soon allayed when those same battle hardened, but disciplined, paratroopers fitted quickly and quietly in to their new surroundings as British soldiers have done for centuries the world over. Naturally, some of the hostelries in the larger towns became the setting for the occasional 'battle-royal' when old scores were settled. One such fracas, remembered by Roy Tyler, took place in Newark shortly after the Division returned to England, when the Paratroopers out on the town noticed that also present were some of the air crews responsible for scattering the Division far and wide over Sicily the previous year. A certain amount of vengeance and retribution was wreaked that night. For the Provost it resulted in two quick postings out of the Company, several Reprimands and, worst punishment of all, a beerless fortnight.

Reinforced and re-equipped, Sections went out on attachment to the Brigades at Woodall Spa and Oakham, training with the various formations, manufacturing and erecting hundreds of semi-permanent unit locations signs along miles of country lanes, and the routine Security and Patrol duties. There were also visits to the Company and the Division by a succession of inquisitive dignitaries, all requiring much spit and polish prior to the big day. Major General R.E. Urquhart DSO had taken over command of the Division on the 7th of January 1944 and paid a visit to the Company at their Stubton HQ on the 3rd of February. There were also two very important visitors to the Division during March which had all the Redcaps out on duty; General (later Field Marshal) Montgomery on the 14th and His Majesty King George VI two days later.

Soon after arriving back in England the Division had been warned to be ready for operations by the end of April. It was obvious that something big was 'on the cards'. Hardwick Hall and the Parachute Training School at Ringway were working at full capacity and those members of the Company who had been attached to the Airlanding Brigade in North Africa, and who had not fully completed their parachute training, were put through the system. Their numbers included the recently promoted Warrant Officer, RSM Martin and Lcpl Peter Dale who, you will recall, had spent the night of 9/10 July 1943 swimming towards the coastline of Sicily when the glider he was travelling in had landed in the sea. Inevitably there were those who volunteered for the Airborne

Provost Company attracted by the glamour and publicity surrounding the Red Beret and the idea of becoming a Paratrooper, only to find that they could not attain the supreme level of physical fitness and dedication required of them. Others passed the fitness training with ease, then balked when it came to the final test at Ringway, the balloon and aircraft jumps.

Under the fatherly guidance, and occasional firm hand, of the experienced Senior Ranks, The Company soon had the North African sand and Italian vino out of its system. Frequent, but brief, 'shake-down' exercises were held to test Sections or half-Sections in driving skills, map reading traffic control, route signing, weapon handling etc. Other exercises involved the Sections operating alongside elements of the Division up to Brigade strength. Jack Coates recalls one such exercise in the Huddersfield area with live firing on the Yorkshire Moors. Another exercise was held around Grimsby and was based on an old railway yard. The MPs slept rough in an old abandoned railway wagon which Jack found good training for his Prisoner of War days to come before the year was out. On that same exercise John Hamblett remembers 'capturing' the local brewery.... but that could be just wishful thinking! Another Section was sent out on exercise which entailed their existing solely on a 48 hour ration pack for the duration. On the second day a Section Mobile Patrol came across a RASC Stores Depot from which they 'obtained' the ingredients for a nourishing stew. The Section Sergeant, honest to the end, refused his share as he said this would be 'cheating'.

Being back in England and billeted tantalisingly close to friends and loved ones in London, Liverpool and Manchester, the temptation for a quick visit home was ever-present. Precious 36 or 48 hour passes could be obtained between duties and exercises, but there was always the problem of transport. Railway tickets cost money which wasn't always available. Hitch hiking was too unreliable and many valuable hours may be wasted waiting for a lift on the A1. There were other methods available which were not always strictly on the right side of King's Regulations but it **was** wartime and, contrary to popular belief, Redcaps were only human. Dennis Riley came from Manchester and the odd pints of petrol 'saved' during the week would get him and his army motor cycle home at weekends, with the bike's Workticket endorsed, 'Special Duties – Preston and Return'. The local REME Workshop ensured that the machine was kept well tuned, and Dennis would turn a blind eye when he saw the REME vehicle parked in a side street near the driver's home. That same REME driver later transferred to the CMP and went to Palestine as a Sergeant.

Fred Weatherley was a Corporal with 21st Independent Parachute Company in 1944. He remembers:

> *We were confined to a 10 mile radius of our camp at the time, which would only allow us to visit Newark or Lincoln from where we could be summoned back to camp relatively quickly. Outside this area it was essential to have an official pass. Needless to say that I had no such pass but was hitch hiking some 25 miles out on the road to Leicester when I spotted an Army Jeep approaching and hailed it hopefully. To my joy it pulled up, but my heart sank when I saw that the driver, and sole occupant, was a Military Police Sergeant. He was well built, red faced with short cropped gingerish hair, and extremely tough looking. He asked me where I was bound and I told him ... "Leicester." He asked for my pass and I had to admit that I didn't have one. He asked me what unit I was from and I told him. He said, ..."I thought you blokes in the 21st had more sense." Then he told me to look under the dashboard where I found a book of blank passes already stamped with the name of some obscure, perhaps even non-existent Airborne unit. The Sergeant told me to fill one in, complete with forged signature, with the admonition... "If you're picked up and spill the beans as to where you got that pass, I'll have your guts for garters."Or words to that effect. He dropped me off in Leicester at the exact spot I wanted to be – my girlfriend's house – and waved away my thanks. I enjoyed my day out and returned to camp OK. There had been no flap and I was in the clear. I never saw the Sergeant again but I often thought of him and hoped that he survived the war.*

(Note: From the description the Sergeant was undoubtedly 'Mac' McKnight who later became RSM of the Company.)

By May the Division was ready for war again. It had re-equipped and re-inforced, exercised in groups, from Section to Division strength, and had pounded practically every mile of the country lanes in Lincolnshire burdened with ever increasing loads. One three day exercise held towards the end of April had the Division acting as enemy to the 6th Airborne Div. in the South of England. Although the troops were unaware at the time, this was a full scale rehearsal for D-Day and the invasion of France some few weeks hence. A group of NCOs with the Airlanding Brigade Provost Section had a lucky escape when their glider made a heavy crash landing near Petersfield. As the glider came to a standstill with the fuselage in tatters, a voice from within shouted ..."Take up all round protection!" Dennis Fitzgerald informed the voice that ...."We're in bloody England and we've just crashed. What do you want all round protection for?"

When the 6th Airborne spearheaded the invasion into Europe there was a great feeling of frustration around Lincolnshire. The 1st Airborne was finely honed, ready for action, and months of intensive training had bought the men to a peak. Now they felt deflated. Understandably, the reaction produced a certain amount of indiscipline within the Division. Fighting, drunkenness and absenteeism were the main problems the Provost Company had to deal with as certain of the Paratroopers vented their frustration. Jack Coates was a member of Number 1 Section attached to the 1st Parachute Brigade. Headquarters for the brigade was at Syston Hall with the Provost billeted at nearby Barkeston from where they would carry out the Brigade HQ Security Duties and patrols of the nearby towns and villages. He remembers:

> *If there was any trouble the main culprits were usually the hard nuts of the 2nd Battalion, many of them little Scotsmen who would fight anybody, for any reason, at the drop of a hat. It was something of a local joke that the boys with the yellow lanyards could always find some excuse to have a go at the American troops, either because the yanks didn't stand up quickly enough when the National Anthem was played in the local Dance hall, or because some imagined, or manufactured, insult to a local girl.*

Instances of absenteeism, or simply returning a day or two late from a weekend pass, rose rapidly within the Division. However, rumours that an Operation was 'on the cards' soon had the miscreants rushing back to join their units. One was even rumoured to have returned by taxi, so eager was he to get in on the action. Others, like Stan Reast of the Div. HQ Provost Section, worked out their frustration by volunteering to help the local farmers around Stubton with their harvesting. It was hot and tiring work throughout the day, but there was always the promise of a few well earned pints in the evening to slake their thirst.

By June the various Provost Sections were billeted close to their respective Brigades, leaving the remaining three Sections at Stubton, Number 1 Section (attached to 1st Parachute Brigade), under Lieutenant Wilf Morley, at Barkeston. Number 2 section (attached to 4th Parachute Brigade), under Lieutenant Frank Locke, in stables at Stapleford Park near Melton Mowbray, Number 3 Section (attached to the Airlanding Brigade), under Lieutenant Frank Horton, at Woodall Spa prior to moving down to the Brize Norton area. Division HQ operated from Fulbeck Hall and the CMP Company HQ Sections provided Security Duties on the main entrance with patrols of the buildings and grounds at night. The Policemen, a half-Section at a time, were accommodated for their period of duty in a tiny two up and two down cottage close to the Hall. (The cottage had hardly changed in 1993 when the authors paid a nostalgic visit to Fulbeck. However, it is now occupied by a smart young businesswoman and echoes to a more ladylike language).

Following the D-Day landings in Normandy on the 6th of June 1944, the first Airborne was held in readiness for possible Operations in support of the Allied advance. Many targets were considered for the Division during June, July and August, but all were cancelled at various stages of the planning as the proposed targets were overrun by our rapidly advancing forces. No fewer than seventeen such Operations were mooted that summer, four of them reaching the stage where the troops were confined to camp, aircraft and gliders were loaded, only to be unloaded again within a few hours. The fortunes of the 6th Airborne and the progress of the invasion force was followed keenly by those left kicking their heels in Lincolnshire, and their spirits sank lower with each cancelled operation. The question on everyone's lips was … "When will it be our turn?"

A problem facing the Div.HQ at this time was one of keeping the possible movement of the Division a secret. It was difficult to impose or implement a security blackout when so many of the 10,000 troops in the area were courting local girls and regularly visiting their homes, frequenting the many local pubs and Dance Halls, or nipping off home on weekend leaves. The warning of the wartime poster that … *'Careless Talk Costs Lives'* … could not have been more appropriate.

Within the Company there had been a major change of personnel. Jock Gray was promoted to Acting Captain and appointed Officer Commanding, a move welcomed throughout the whole Company. Captain Gray had been with the unit almost from its formation when he had joined from the CMP Depot. He had been a popular Warrant Officer, guiding the fledgling NCOs through the past two years and had well deserved his emergency commission the previous year. His manner was firm but friendly, strict yet approachable, and with a Liverpool streak of humour. A few well chosen words or a quip often defused an awkward situation or released the tension under the most testing conditions.

In the meantime, whilst operations were being planned and cancelled with frustrating regularity, the phlegmatic British soldier opted to enjoy life while he could – or at least the Redcaps did. Time was short, something had to happen soon, and life was lived if not on a knife-edge, then certainly half way down the handle. Number 3 Section with the Airlanding Brigade somehow managed to acquire a goat as a Section mascot. The goat would accompany Dennis Fitzgerald on patrol in the 15cwt truck, sitting in the passenger seat and peering through the window. When the Section left for Arnhem, 'Billy' was handed over to the KOSB Rear Party. Dennis hopes that it lived out it's life and didn't end as a dish on the Cookhouse menu.

Impromptu nights down at the Five Bells public house in Claypole were organised with a sing-song and a trip to the local Fish and Chip shop before the long walk back to camp. Harry Wilce remembers those innocent nights down at the pub, and the 'competition' on the way back to Stubton to see who could stay longest on the back of a cow in a field. There was also one particular NCO, a REME 'Tiffy' attached to the Company, who had annoyed the returning revellers in some respect. He was promptly stripped down to his birthday suit, tied firmly to his bed, and carried through the night to be deposited on the front lawn of the Women's Land Army accommodation at the Stubton Rectory. It was reported that the elderly Miss in charge of the girls almost passed out when confronted by the shivering 'Tiffy' at daybreak.

There were also incidents of a certain RSM's pace-stick being cut in to small pieces and handed out as souvenirs, of a piano being manhandled out of a public house in Witney by a group of off-duty MPs and Glider Pilots, and of 'spending a penny' from a glider passing over Grantham. But, as the perpetrator of the last incident had a successful post-war career in the Constabulary, and is still living in the rudest of health and a fine pillar of his community, the details will be glossed over. After all, it *was* wartime.

It was thought a certainty that the Division would be committed into the battle for Europe before the summer was out, but exactly when and where had yet to be decided. Caen, Falaise, the area south of Paris and Tournai had all been planned and cancelled as the mighty invasion force thrust remorselessly inland towards Germany. In early August the decision was taken to send a Divisional Seaborne Element into the Normandy beachhead ahead of any future Airborne element. This Seaborne party would take the bulk of the Division's vehicles loaded with spare ammunition, fuel, sleeping bags, clothing and other essential stores. The convoy was to leave England in two groups with the first, the largest, sailing on the 14th August, and the second to follow at a date to be decided once the Airborne Element had been committed.

Two CMP Sections were detailed to travel with the first Seaborne party, one Section to carry out all convoy escort and route signing duties, and the second Section to travel as part of the convoy with the Provost vehicles and stores. The NCOs from each of the Brigade Provost Sections nominated for the Seaborne Element concentrated at Company HQ at Stubton and by Saturday the 12th August all was loaded and ready for the off. John Hamblett was one of two Corporals detailed for the Duty Section and recalls:

Captain Gray decided that as many of the Company as possible would gather at the nearby Railway pub in Claypole for a farewell drink on the eve of the Seaborne Element's departure. The village had never seen so many laden military vehicles converge on it at one time. That night there was much beer drunk, songs sung, and stories told before we all staggered back to our billets. We were not to know that this would be the last time that the whole Company would be together. Reveille the next morning was at 3am and the Company was woken not by the gentle sounds of the Lincolnshire countryside, nor the ringing notes of the military bugle, but by the RSM entering each of the Nissen huts and firing off a few rounds from his Sten gun in to the air. The racket soon got rid of any thick heads and hangovers from the night before. At 4.30 in the morning the friendly village of Stubton saw the departure of our convoy of vehicles, waved off by the rest of the Company HQ NCOs as we left to join up with the main body of the Seaborne Element. Everyone was in excellent spirits at the prospect of what lay ahead and the fact that our long period of inactivity in Lincolnshire was finally at an end. Little did we realise what frustrations, disappointments and disasters the future held for our mates in the Airborne Element.

After the departure of the Seaborne convoy the remainder of the Company carried on with their routine duties, still patiently waiting to be committed to the fierce battle raging across the English Channel. They were not to be kept waiting for very much longer.

By late August the German armies were in full retreat towards their own country as more than a million Allied troops fought their way out of the congested Normandy bridgeheads and swept forward in a fury of controlled vengeance in pursuit of the enemy. Paris was liberated on the 23rd of August, followed by Brussels by the Guards Armoured Division on the 4th September as the British and American Armies surged forward. By the time they reached the Belgian/Dutch border the momentum had slowed down considerably. The supply lines stretched for over 300 miles back to Cherbourg and the artificial port constructed at Arromanches.

Petrol, food, ammunition, clothing, spare parts all had to be moved forward by road and the front line units found themselves desperately short of these vital commodities.

Ahead of the Allies lay the path to Germany's back door. A rapid advance along the route, Eindhoven-Grave-Nijmegen and Arnhem would allow the Allies to by-pass the German West Wall or Siegfried Line and strike eastwards into the industrial heart of Germany. But before the advance could begin the Allies had to seize control of the many bridges crossing the canals and rivers along the route. These included the large road bridge spanning the River Maas at Grave, that crossing the River Waal at Nijmegen, and the most northerly bridge over the Lower Rhine at Arnhem.

On the 6th of September 1944 the Division was warned for Operation Comet. This ambitious plan gave each of the three Brigades of the Division the task of capturing and holding one of the main bridges. Could this, at last, be the opportunity everyone had been waiting for? Again, aircraft and gliders were meticulously checked and loaded, detailed briefings were held and the troops confined to camps close to the departure airfields. But the delay forced upon the Allies in Belgium had allowed the enemy to regroup, reinforce and put up a stiff resistance. Operation Comet was cancelled on the 10th September.

The following day Operation Market-Garden was announced and was to be put in to operation just 5 days later on the 17th of September. The revised plan allocated the major bridge objectives, and the roads linking them, not to one but to three Airborne Divisions. The American 101st, (Eindhoven to Grave), the American 82nd, (Grave to Nijmegen), and the British 1st Airborne, (the road bridge at Arnhem some 64 miles behind the German lines). In effect the three Divisions would lay down an airborne 'carpet' along which the advancing Allies would race towards Germany led by 30 Corps with the tanks of the Irish Guards as the spearhead. 'MARKET' was the Airborne part of the Operation, and 'GARDEN' the ground forces thrust.

Back with the Provost Company in England, RSM Martin had sustained an injury in a parachute accident and his place was taken by ex-Grenadier, Bill Kibble. The Sections attached to the Brigades had been together, with only the occasional inter-Section posting of individual NCOs, since returning from North Africa. Over the months they had been blended in to close knit teams and were as ready for action as they ever would be. Each Section was led by a Lieutenant, but guided by the older, experienced Section Sergeant. Jack Coates was a Lance Corporal with Number 1 Section and he remembered:

> Our Sergeant was 'Cab' Calloway, a fine man and a great bloke to be with. He was firm and definitely in charge of the Section. Nobody messed around with 'Cab', but at the same time he was one of the boys, a man you could talk to and rely on.

Before the month was out those Section Sergeants and their young NCO charges were to be put to the severest of tests. Many would not survive, but none would be found wanting.

The days leading to 'Market-Garden' were hectic with numerous briefings, kit to be packed and re-packed, last letters home to be written, maps to be carefully studied and grid references, code words and RV points to be memorised. All troops were confined to their camps with public telephone boxes sealed or guarded by Military Police to prevent a possible indiscreet or compromising last minute telephone call being made to a loved one. Gliders were carefully loaded and balanced under the keen eye of the Glider Pilot. Individual aircraft were checked and re-checked. Were the anchor cables and strops properly secured? Had all the projections and sharp edges on the exit doors been masked with tape? Surely there couldn't be another cancellation now!

The shortage of aircraft meant that the Division had to be flown in to Arnhem over three days, commencing on Sunday the 17th. Take off would be from a total of 22 British and American airfields stretching from Dorset to Lincolnshire, and the planned order of arrival was:

1st Lift. Sunday 17th   21 Indep. Para Company
                                  Part of Div. HQ
                                  1st Parachute Brigade
                                  Majority of 1st Airlanding Brigade

        2 x Field Ambulance Units
        Support Troops
        Part of 4th Parachute Bde.

2nd Lift. Monday 18th 4th Parachute Brigade
        Remainder of Div. HQ
        Remainder of Airlanding Brigade
        Field Ambulance Unit
        Support Troops

3rd Lift. Tuesday 19th 1st Polish Parachute Brigade*
*Actually arrived on 21st due to bad weather in England.

  In the 24 hours before Sunday the 17th German flak positions, airfields, barracks and coastal batteries along the flight path were systematically attacked by waves of Allied fighter and bomber aircraft. Allocated for the first lift of the Division were 143 Dakotas to carry parachutists and 358 tug aircraft, (Sterlings, Albermarles, Halifaxes and Dakotas), to bring in 345 Horsa gliders and 13 of the larger Hamilcars. The gliders would lift off from airfields around Oxfordshire and Gloucestershire while the Dakotas carrying the Paratroopers took off from around Grantham.

  All was now ready and the Lincolnshire interval was rapidly drawing to a close. The disappointment of seeing their sister Division, the 6th, chosen for the Normandy landings and the anti-climax of so many false alarms and cancelled operations was behind them. At last it was their turn.

  At Stubton Hall, Barkeston, Stapleford Park and Brize Norton, the NCOs of the various Provost Sections went to bed in their billets, for some it would be the last time under an English moon. Some would not sleep as free men for many months to come, others were tasting their final hours of an English autumn.

  They woke to a 5am Reveille, Sunday the 17th dawned bright and clear and the forecast promised a fine sunny September day.

Map 2
The Battle of Arnhem
Dropping and Landing Zones

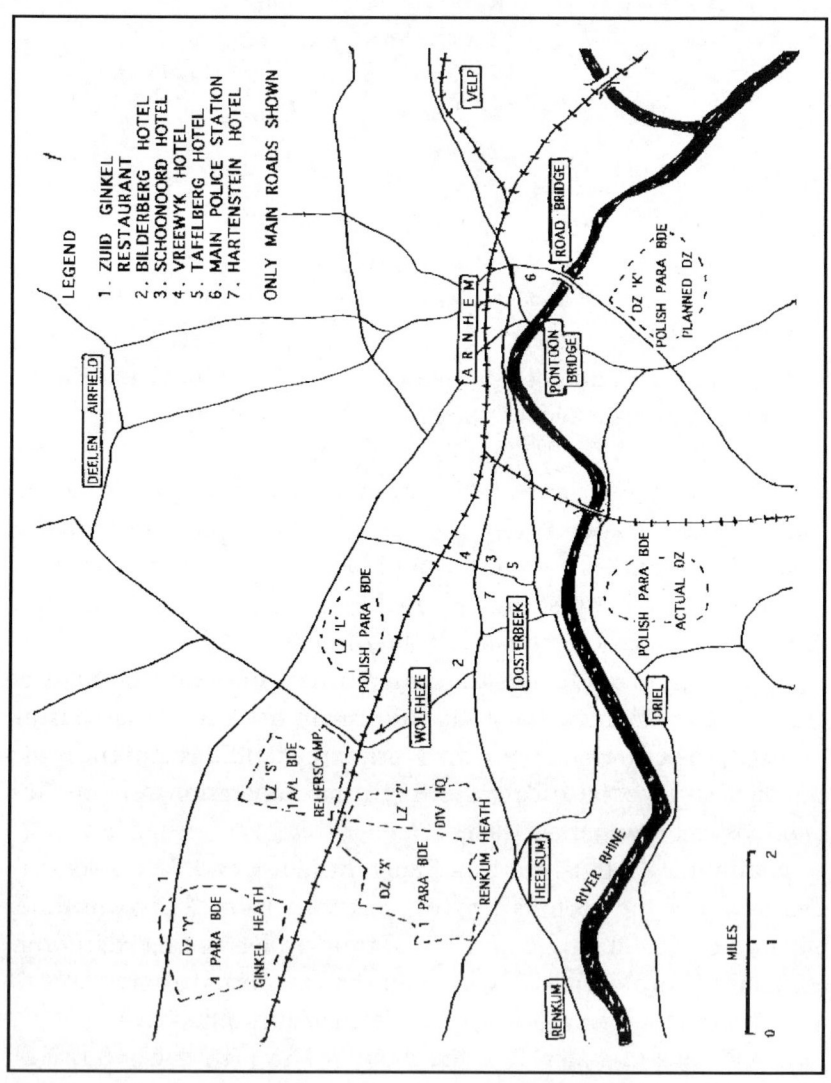

CHAPTER 4

NUMBER 1 SECTION (ATT. 1ST PARACHUTE BRIGADE)

It was quiet in the town and it seemed like we'd cracked it
(Lcpl Jack Coates at the Arnhem Police Station, 17th September)

Lance Corporal Jack Coates rolled up his sleeping bag and placed it with his kitbag of spare clothing at the foot of his bed. They would be brought out to Holland in a week or so once 30 Corps had linked up with the Division at Arnhem. He dressed quickly but carefully, not wanting to be the last in the breakfast queue. Over his rough khaki battledress he wore the familiar windproof camouflage smock. His webbing equipment, carefully adjusted for the maximum comfort, was fitted over the smock together with his accoutrements of battle. Finally he struggled in to the web harness onto which he would clip his parachute when the time came.

Number 1 Section, led by Lieutenant Wilf Morley of the Parachute Regiment paraded beside the transport which was to take them to the airfield. Under the critical eye of Sergeant 'Cab' Calloway they formed into three ranks for inspection. Corporal Jim Peers from Port Sunlight along with Lance Corporals Coates, Cox, Fantarrow, Keddie, McGaw, McIntosh, Phillips, Pummell, Whitmill, Wilkinson, Wright and the Canadian 'Canada' Young. The second Section Corporal, Harold Bennett was to travel by glider on the 18th with the Section Jeep and trailer. Before the week was out one of their number would be lying dead in an Arnhem street, whilst another would be hiding from the enemy.

The inspection completed, the NCOs collected their parachutes and made their way towards the transport. There was the usual nervous banter between the friends as the trucks drove through the still deserted village streets for the short journey to the airfield at Barkeston Heath.

The airfield was already swarming with men and machines at that early hour of the morning. Row upon serried row of Dakotas, noses pointing towards the sky as though eager to be airborne, convoys of trucks disgorging thousands of paratroopers. Groups of men fussed around each of the aircraft carrying out last minute checks or making final adjustments to the load. There were still three hours to go before take-off and the NCOs stretched out on the grass beside the runway, warming themselves in the early morning sunshine, some enjoying a cigarette and chatting in groups, others lying quietly with their own private thoughts. The military administrative machine had not overlooked the tea-wagon in all its planning, and this duly arrived at 10am on the dot to dole out sweet tea and sandwiches.

Half an hour later the order was given to emplane. Bodies rose from the grass, parachutes were clipped in to place and lines of men, burdened under all their kit and equipment, shuffled towards their allocated aircraft and helped each other aboard.

Lance Corporals Jock Keddie and Mick Cox were in the same stick as Lt Morley. When the stick numbers had been drawn Mick had drawn number 13, and Jock number 12. Mick was a Dubliner, a staunch Roman Catholic, and more than a little superstitious. He begged his mate Jock to swap numbers with him, but Jock was having none of it. Fingers tightly crossed throughout the flight, a few mumbled 'Hail Mary's ' did the trick and both made safe landings on the DZ.

Soon after 11 o'clock the peace of that Sunday morning was shattered as the twin engines of each Dakota were started up and given a brief test at full throttle. Then the planes trundled forward to line up, packed tightly together, at the end of the runway waiting for the signal to go. The first flight of three aircraft lifted off shortly after 11.30am to be rapidly followed by flight after flight at fifteen second intervals until the air above Grantham was a mass of circling Dakotas. Similar formations were lifting off from other airfields around Lincolnshire before joining into one massive fleet of aircraft heading towards the channel coast.

Jack Coates has vivid memories of the flight:

> *Our aircraft was in the first wave heading for Arnhem. It was an uneventful flight and we were much assured by the flocks of friendly fighters which accompanied us on our way. There was a bit of flak as we flew over Holland, with the odd pieces of shrapnel rattling and tinkling on the side of the fuselage, but it all seemed fairly harmless. Anyway, we were all convinced that the Germans were washed-up and finished. (Oh how one deludes oneself!) I was airsick on the way over, the first and only time that I ever had that problem. I still cannot say if it was caused by the turbulence, or whether I was just scared stiff. It was about 1.15pm when we arrived over the DZ and the weather was perfect. There were thousands of Paras floating down as we leapt out of the aircraft to join them. Apart from some small arms fire rattling away in the distance there was no opposition to speak of. We had jumped with the new style kitbags strapped to our left legs. These contained additional equipment and stores and were released on the end of a thirty foot rope on the way down. When the kitbag hit the deck it gave a slight lift to the parachute and made for a gentle landing.*

Jock Keddie was in another aircraft and had very good reasons to remember his own particular drop that day:

> *Over the DZ I was glad to be out of the aircraft and into the fresh air. Seconds after I jumped something whistled past me. I thought at first that it was Mick Cox who was jumping after me, but when I landed I found that it had been a radio set which somebody had dropped. On the way down it was a silent and peaceful as you could wish for. I remember looking down and seeing a neat little house with a fence around it and a cow running around in a small field. The cow had these long horns which were sticking in to the air. I thought to myself ... "If you land on those horns you'll be in trouble". ... My main concern was to avoid the cow.*

The DZ had been marked with coloured smoke by members of the 21st Independent Parachute Company and the Section quickly joined up at the pre-arranged RV. Lance Corporal Pummell had unfortunately suffered a broken arm on landing and was left in the care of the Medics on the DZ. The Brigade Operation Order tasked the CMP with providing guides to direct the transport being unloaded from the gliders to the various unit assembly areas, and to point the descending paratroopers towards their Company or Battalion RVs. With these tasks completed the Section were to head straight for Arnhem, some 8 miles away, to take over the main Civilian Police Station in the centre of the town, and to hold it until the arrival of the relieving 30 Corps which was expected within 48 hours. In addition, Lt. Wilf Morley and one NCO, (Lcpl Jock Keddie), were to head for the main Arnhem road bridge where they were to pick up a Dutch Army officer who would interrogate any prisoners held in the Police Station.

On the edge of the DZ the Section took charge of a small group of bewildered and demoralised German prisoners who had been captured by the first Paras to land. Together captives and captors set off on that pleasant Sunday afternoon in the direction of Arnhem. They had landed on an area of open heath between the village of Heelsum and the main Arnhem/Utrecht railway and followed, fortunately as it transpired, the route taken by Lt. Colonel Frost's 2nd Battalion, 'Lion Route'. Open farmland gradually gave way to the trim suburbs of Heelsum, Doorwerth and Oosterbeek with their quiet tree-lined avenues and graceful houses standing in neat gardens. At Oosterbeek the file of Redcaps turned right and dropped down towards the River Rhine, then followed the road leading towards town.

Approaching Arnhem in the gathering dusk along the lower road the Section surprised a member of the 2nd Battalion who was sheltering in the doorway of a house. He was Private Robert Peatling of the Battalion Signals Platoon who had become separated whilst out on patrol. He tells what happened next:

> *I heard the sound of marching feet and crossed to the doorway of a house facing the river. I saw what was obviously our chaps with a sergeant leading a column in single file. He*

told me that he had not passed anyone else on the lower road so I decided to return to the bridge with him. It was a Military Police Section with 20 prisoners and they were heading for the Armhem Police Station. I took up the rearguard and was going to drop off as soon as we were challenged by the 2nd Battalion. On the way we picked up Sgt. Harry Parker of the 3rd Battalion and, on our eventual arrival at the Police Station we said that we were off to the main bridge and our proper positions. A Military Police Lieutenant said that we must wait there until he sent an escort for us both, and then he left.

J.D. van Maris was an Arnhem Police Lieutenant during the war. Holland had been under German occupation for a number of years and the Police had been forced to adopt military titles. In his comprehensive report on the events of that evening he writes:

They, (the CMP Section plus Peatling and Parker), walked about for some time until they saw a dim light in a large building. They entered the building and found that it was the Control Centre of the Town's Civil Defence, housed in the basement of the Industrial School for Girls. Inside were men of the Civil Defence and representatives of the Fire Department, Public Utilities, Police etc. One of those present was Police Lieutenant Perdijk who, learning that the soldier's destination was the Police Station, expressed his willingness to lead them there. He didn't know anything about the situation in town. He had seen English soldiers passing the Civil Defence building and knew that the St. Elizabeth Hospital in the Western Sector off Arnhem near Oosterbeek was in English hands, and that led him to the conclusion that liberation of the town was only a matter of hours away. Therefore he didn't think there would be any danger and calmly walked with his party through the dark streets to the Police Station on Bovenbeekstraat in the heart of the city. During the walk they did not meet anybody and arrived at about 11pm. The Englishmen were greeted enthusiastically by the Policemen on duty, who then searched the Germans and locked then up in the cells with great satisfaction. The Dutch prisoners held in the Police Station were transferred to cells in another part of the building. The airborne soldiers shared out their cigarettes and chocolate with the Dutch Policemen, a treat which we had not had for years, and the Police provided blankets when the soldiers said that they were tired and wanted to sleep. The Paras wrapped themselves in the blankets and slept on the floor in the cell building, untroubled all through the night. Their Sergeant laid himself down to sleep just behind the door so that nobody could enter without awakening him.

The Police Station, which also served as the Police HQ for Arnhem, was a large rectangular, red-brick building of two storeys and an attic. There was a courtyard to one side where the Police transport was parked. The courtyard was overlooked by windows from inside the Station and could be entered via an iron gate from the street. Inside on that Sunday evening all was relatively calm and peaceful. The German prisoners were just as exhausted as the Section NCOs and were happy to be in a 'safe' place as they settled down for the night. Jack Coates again:

It was quiet in the town and it seemed that we had cracked it. All we had to do was dig in and hold out for a couple of days until we were relieved by the 2nd Army coming up from the South. How were we to know that they hadn't a hope in hell of reaching us in such a short time.

On the following morning, Monday the 18th, a different picture presented itself. Sounds of a heavy battle could be heard quite clearly and the streets around the Police Station were swarming with heavily armed German soldiers. It was learnt from the Dutch Policemen that there was fighting taking place around the St. Elizabeth Hospital and that only the north end of the bridge was in British hands.

For the Dutch Policemen this presented an awkward and embarrassing problem. Lt van Maris explained the dilemma in his report:

The Dutch Police Commander sent out a patrol and when the men came back they reported that the roads to Oosterbeek and the Rhinebridge were full of SS troops. They realised that if the Germans recaptured the Police Station it would put them in an awkward position as they would have to explain why they had locked up the German soldiers without warning the German Military Staff. After consultation with the Military Police Sergeant the Dutch Policemen decided to sneak out of the Police Station. As a precaution the arrival of the British had not been mentioned in the Police report of the previous night. Opposite the Police Station there was a building which was also used by the Police. In the back yard there was an underground shelter and at about 8am the whole Police Force went in to the shelter after having first released all the Dutch prisoners from the cells. That same morning they left the shelter in small groups and went home. That was the end of the Arnhem Police for nearly six months.

Map 3
Arnhem Bridge showing, (inset), the proximity of the main police station.

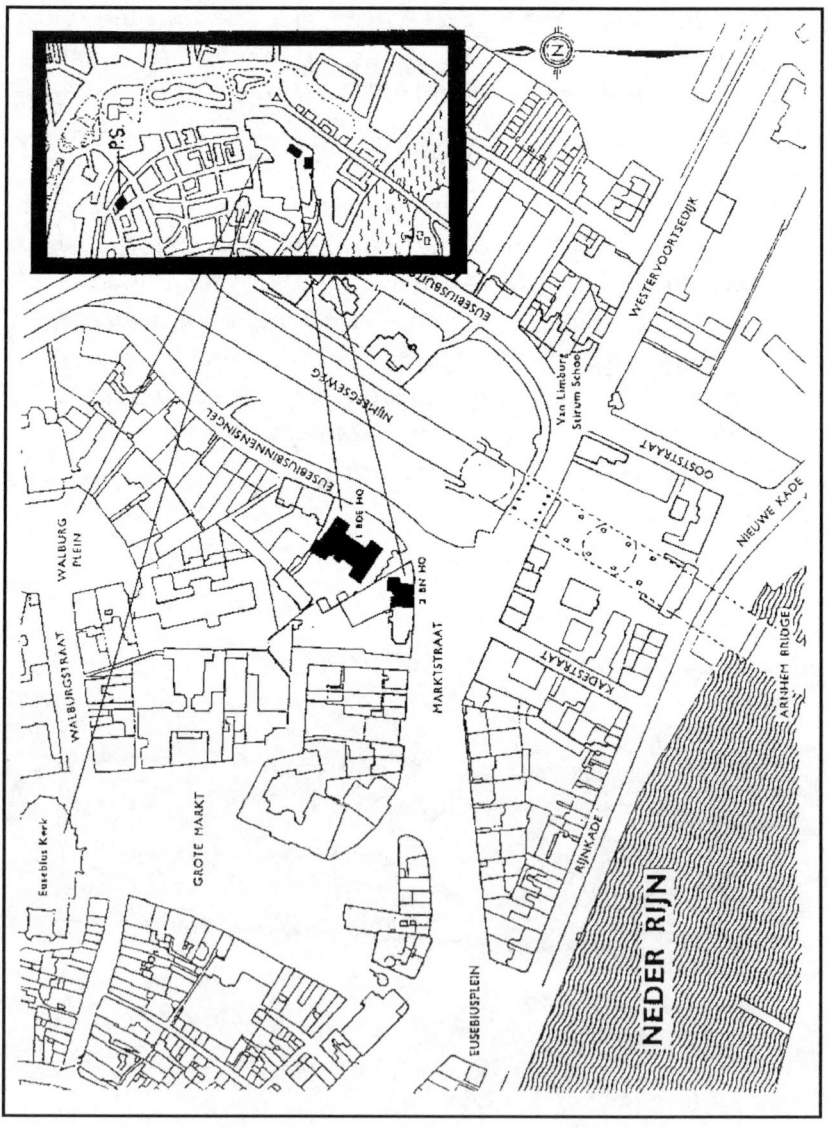

No 1 Section (1st Parachute Brigade)

Sergeant Calloway took stock of their situation. He had one of his Section Corporals, a handful of Lance Corporals, plus Bob Peatling and Harry Parker. As yet the enemy were unaware that the Section had occupied the Police Station – but for how long? Each of the Military Policemen was armed with a Sten gun, a few spare magazines of ammunition and a couple of hand grenades each. Peatling and Parker had their rifles. Ammunition was ample for the time being, but there was a shortage of food. The rations which the soldiers carried with them, together with the meagre supplies found in the Police Station, would have to be shared with the 20 prisoners until 2nd Army arrived.

The NCOs were detailed off to defensive positions inside the building, some guarding the German prisoners and others on watch at the windows overlooking the surrounding streets. It was 8.30am on Monday the 18th September, the sound of heavy fighting could be heard around the Police Station and the Redcaps settled down to watch and wait.

Meanwhile, what of Lt. Morley and Lcpl Keddie. Their orders had been to make straight for the main bridge, pick up the Dutch Army Officer and take him to the Police Station where he would interrogate the Dutch prisoners held there. Morley and Keddie had left the DZ on the Sunday and reached the bridge in the early evening. There they headed for the building earmarked as Brigade HQ where they met up with the Dutch Officer and the three of them set off for the Police Station. Jock Keddie continues:

> On the way through the streets to the Police Station we came under sniper fire. The Dutch Officer was either killed or very badly wounded and I never saw him again. Lt. Morley and I made our way slowly back to the bridge, getting stopped every now and then by Paras demanding the Password. We eventually got back to the bridge and reported to Brigade HQ. During the evening more and more Paras were coming into the building. A Sergeant there was organising the defence of the HQ and I was detailed to stand guard on the main door. Lt. Morley had gone off somewhere, I think back to the Police Station to see how the rest of the Section were getting on. I stayed on guard at the door into the early hours

of the morning until Lt. Morley returned and the two of us went upstairs and took up positions at the windows. We stayed there until it became light the following morning.

By dawn on Monday the northern end of the bridge, and the surrounding buildings, were occupied by about 500 British. These comprised almost two Companies of 2nd Parachute Battalion, Brigade HQ (less Brigadier Lathbury), elements of RASC, RE and a small number of the Recce Squadron. Close artillery support consisted of 4 x 6 pounder anti-tank guns with their crews. The defenders had also to contend with almost 100 German prisoners held in the cellars of the buildings, who had been captured the previous evening as the paras fought to secure their foothold on the end of the bridge. The remainder of the 1st Parachute Brigade had run into stiff opposition on their way to the bridge and had been prevented from joining up with the 2nd Battalion.

The defenders stood-to at first light, alert in their buildings and slit trenches for the inevitable German response. It wasn't long in coming. Lorries full of apprehensive Panzer Grenadiers drove slowly through the streets into the midst of the waiting Paras. The British held their fire until the last moment then a hail of bullets tore into the unfortunate Grenadiers. Most of them were killed in the storm of machine gun and rifle bullets, and the rest were captured.

The enemy's next attack came from south of the river in the form of a convoy of 16 armoured cars and half-tracks which attempted to drive across the bridge and into the town behind the British. Again, the line of vehicles were allowed to drive into the waiting Para's ambush. The leading armoured cars accelerated over the bridge and onto the sloping roadway passing through the British positions and into the town. At a given signal, from their positions in trenches beside the road, from rooftops, doorways, balconies and windows the defenders poured everything they had at the vehicles and their crews. Rifles, machine guns, hand grenades, PIAT bombs and shell after shell from the 6 pounders soon reduced the convoy to a flaming mass of wrecked machinery. As Colonel Frost was later to report ... "there was no exemption from the firing line, all ranks and trades were in it, Staff Officers, signallers, batmen, drivers and clerks."

No 1 Section (1st Parachute Brigade)

Jock Keddie had become part of that firing line too, his Military Police duties forgotten. He was now another valuable body able to squeeze a trigger amongst the ever-diminishing band of stalwart paratroopers. Following the abortive attack by the German convoy yet more prisoners were collected to swell the numbers already held. Keddie remembers:

They took the prisoners downstairs, including a couple of German Officers. I escorted them down the stairs and put them in one of the rooms. I stayed guarding the prisoners throughout most of the Monday. At the height of all this, with all the shelling and shooting going on all around us, a Dutch Policeman walked casually in to the building. How on earth he made it through the streets I don't know, but he came in to make a complaint about something or other. Anyway, he was sent on his way. Then they started bringing in our own wounded lads. There was a medical Corps Aid Post in the same building and the cellars were pretty soon crammed with both prisoners and wounded.

From their defensive positions at the Police Station the Military Policemen peered cautiously through the windows at the enemy activity in the streets below. It would only be a matter of time before their presence in the building was discovered. Jack Coates and Bernard Phillips were positioned at the entrance to the Cell Block on the ground floor guarding the prisoners. They also had a clear view in to the courtyard and the main entrance from the street. Jack Coates again:

When we reviewed the situation on the Monday it looked a bit grim. We appeared to be on an 'island' formed by streets on three sides, isolated from the rest of the airborne troops and with not the slightest idea of what was going on outside. Even worse was the fact that the German soldiers were running up and down outside the Police Station calling and shouting to each other clearly believing that they were in total command of the situation. There was a regular stream in and out of the Station of who we took to be Dutch Police

Officers, both in uniform and civilian clothes. We didn't know if they were German sympathisers and might report our presence to the enemy. We questioned those who could speak English about the state of the battle, but received very little information except that there was very heavy fighting down at the bridge.

'Bull' Phillips and I shared what water and small amount of rations we had with the prisoners. 'Bull' established some sort of rapport with one of them, an elderly Feldwebel. They had both been in North Africa and shared a few words and phrases of French. The Feldwebel was able to quieten his fellow-prisoners who were starting to get a bit restless and unruly. This was not surprising considering the lack of food and being locked in a cell when all hell was likely to break loose at any moment. They could also hear their comrades outside in the street and were trying to attract their attention by shouting at the tops of their voices. I had to adopt a nasty, mean paratrooper stance as I cocked my Sten and thrust it through the cell bars in a threatening manner to shut them up. They quietened down for a while, but they needn't have worried. I had no intention of massacring a cell full of unarmed men. Some time during that day Sergeant Callaway came in to the cell block to see us and say that we were going to try and make a break for it that night. But, by the time it got dark the situation appeared completely hopeless. Every time we moved a burst of gunfire came at us from somewhere. That was also the last time I saw 'Cab' alive.

Throughout that Monday there was continuous enemy activity around the Police Station as heavily armed SS troops moved cautiously through the streets heading towards the bridge. The Military Policemen inside the building had long since realised that their enemy wasn't simply the 'old men and invalids' they had expected to encounter. They were up against seasoned and battle hardened veterans. Some time during the afternoon a German soldier passing the Station smashed a ground floor window and snatched a pack lying on a table. The NCO inside the room raised his Sten, but to his amazement, the German had not spotted him and ran off down the street with his booty. Inside the pack was the NCO's food supply. On another occasion an elderly German soldier wandered off the street and into the Station courtyard where he calmly started tinkering with one of the Dutch police cars parked there. He was spotted by Lcpl Wally Whitmill who fired off a burst from his Sten narrowly missing the German who beat a rapid and frightened retreat back into the street.

Still unaware of the situation in the town the Redcaps prepared to make their breakout that night. Their last instructions from Sgt Calloway had been to prepare to move out at midnight. They would attempt to either get through to the bridge, or to try and link up with other friendly forces. Blankets were torn into strips ready to be wrapped around their boots, and weapons were carefully checked in readiness. From the Dutch Policemen who had visited the station during the day they knew that the position was worsening and that the fighting had intensified both at the bridge and in the area of St Elizabeth Hospital. There had been no reassuring news of the relieving 30 Corps, and no contact with their Section Commander, Lt. Morley, since the previous evening.

In the total confusion which prevailed, Sgt. Calloway's movements that Monday afternoon and evening are uncertain. The NCOs in the Police Station were scattered throughout the building, either singly or in pairs, so it was possible that 'Cab' had found himself a window on the upper floors to observe the enemy below. Jack Coates thinks that he may have gone, ..."Scouting around to try and make sense out of the confused situation" .... It is also possible that, shielded by the smoke from the many burning buildings and the confusion in the town, 'Cab' made his way to the bridge to liaise with Lt. Morley. Mike Shardlow was a member of 2nd Battalion and recalls meeting a Military Police Sergeant close to the bridge:

> *I was helping to carry one of our wounded into the Regimental Aid Post at the rear of 2 Para HQ and he was standing at the door. He was a craggy faced chap wearing a beret with a CMP badge, and clutching a Sten. As we carried the wounded man in he said, ... "Well done lads" ... The other man with me said to the CMP Sergeant ... "Stick me on*

a 252 Sarge and send me 'ome"... To which the Sergeant said with a grin ... "Sorry son, I've used 'em all up".

Whether that Sergeant was 'Cab' or Sgt Ernie Howard from the Div. HQ Section is not certain. The facts are that, for whatever reason 'Cab' did not put into effect the planned escape from the Police Station that night and the weary NCOs were faced with another night guarding their prisoners and waiting for relief.

Lt. Morley and Jock Keddie had spent the day in defence of Brigade HQ under constant attack. Keddie looked through the remains of a shattered window down in to a trench occupied by a small group of Paratroopers. He watched a mortar bomb arc through the air and land in the trench beside a young Officer and explode with a deafening roar. The wounded Officer was carried into the room where Keddie was and laid on the floor with the other wounded. The RAMC Doctor gave him an injection, glanced over at Keddie and shook his head slowly. Although there didn't appear to be a mark on the wounded Officer he died within the hour.

The buildings occupied by the handful of Paras came under incessant attack from German artillery and infantry. The crash of falling masonry mingled with the constant crackle of gunfire as individual houses, and even rooms, were fought over with savage ferocity. The dead and wounded of both sides lay where they had fallen in the rubble strewn streets. Evening bought little respite as the area was illuminated in the glow of the many fires.

Tuesday the 19th saw the Germans intensify their attacks on the defenders of the bridge. Although the Paras were well barricaded in their buildings they were no match for the heavy self-propelled guns and tanks which roamed the narrow streets blasting high explosive and phosphorus shells into each building in turn. Gaping holes appeared in the walls exposing the shattered remains of someone's furniture and treasured possessions. Clouds of choking plaster dust filled the air along with the acrid stench of fires and cordite.

Through the crackling and intermittent radio link the remainder of the Division, fighting a desperate battle to get through to the bridge, had been made aware of the plight of the few Paratroopers hanging on grimly to its northern end. A valiant attempt was made to reinforce the 2nd Battalion by fresh troops from the recently landed 2nd Lift, but the attempt failed. The handful of defenders were ordered to hold on and await the expected advance of 30 Corps.

During the morning of the 19th, around 50 enemy artillery men were captured and taken to the Brigade HQ building to join the other prisoners being guarded by Jock Keddie in the cellars. These new prisoners were from a V2 Rocket unit and, with thoughts of the devastation inflicted on London by these weapons, they were understandably nervous in case the Paras discovered their unit. Fortunately for the artillery men the British remained ignorant.

Breakfast at the Police Station on that Tuesday consisted of a cup of tea and a few spoons full of soup shared with the German prisoners. Lt. van Maris takes up the story:

> *The prisoners were becoming restless again and lifted up one of their number so that he could break the small window in the cell and shout to their troops in the street outside. Two Dutch Police Constables visited the Station with news that was not very encouraging. The rest of the Division were pinned down near the St. Elizabeth Hospital, those at the bridge were surrounded, and there was no news of the 2nd Army. There was also disturbing news that the Germans were carrying out house to house searches throughout the town. The Dutchmen left with the promise to return that evening with food. From their windows in the Police Station the British soldiers watched as German soldiers and Dutch civilians looted nearby shops. One of the Germans stopped by the entrance to the Station courtyard and tried to climb over the gate. The Military Policemen positioned at the ground floor window overlooking the gate fired and hit the German in the shoulder. The German dropped down and ran away, and the British now awaited an attack. Shortly afterwards two Dutch civilians entered the building with their arms full of loot from the shops. They were taken prisoner by the British, but eventually released when they promised to return with food.*

At about this time Sgt. Callaway and one of the NCOs climbed onto the flat roof of the Police Station to try to get a better picture of what was happening in the town, and decide if it would be possible for the Section to still get through to the bridge. They crawled along the roof on their stomachs and peered over the edge. To their left they saw a group of German soldiers standing at a road junction. The temptation was too great and a burst from a Sten scattered the Germans. 'Cab' and the NCO hurried down from the roof, but the enemy must have realised where the shooting had come from. Not very long afterwards the Police Station was stormed by SS troops.

Jack Coates and 'Bull' Phillips were on the ground floor guarding the prisoners when the SS raced in through the main entrance and courtyard, firing from all weapons and tossing hand grenades. It was a painful experience for the 21 year old Lcpl Coates and the details of that day are firmly embedded in his memory:

It was about 4.30 in the afternoon when the young SS stormed in. The German prisoners were going berserk in their cells, shouting to their compatriots to hold their fire. There was only one thing for it, that was to open the cell doors and set them free. This created a diversion as they surged along the cell passage and out in to the courtyard, all shouting at the tops of their voices. There was no means of escape from the cell block or the Police Station, we were outnumbered and outgunned, and had no alternative but to follow the prisoners out with our hands in the air. The rest of the Section were forced to come out from their various posts and the German troops lined us up along the wall of the main building. I am pretty sure that we all had the same thought, that the SS were going to shoot us down there and then. Our former prisoners were still milling about in the courtyard, and the elderly Feldwebel was addressing the incoming soldiers, gesticulating in our direction and apparently telling our captors that we weren't really bad fellows. Whatever he said it must have worked because we were eventually marched away out of the Police Station and off to a nearby German HQ.

In the total confusion when the SS stormed the building three of the defenders managed to escape, Sgt Harry Parker from the 3rd Battalion, Lcpl Wally Whitmill CMP, and Pte. Bob Peatling of the 2nd Battalion. Parker and Whitmill went their separate ways as they fled the firing, hiding in the building until darkness gave them cover to dodge away through the streets. Bob Peatling raced up the narrow stairs to the attic and hid amongst the rafters. Through sheer guts, determination and a will to survive he remained in the attic until 31st of October when he was discovered by the Police Lieutenant J.D. van Maris who helped him to escape.

During those hectic few minutes in and around the courtyard, Sgt 'Cab' Callaway was shot dead. The evidence concerning the exact circumstances of his death are contradictory. What is certain is the fact that he was the sort of leader who would have put up a fight, albeit that the small Section were completely outnumbered and surrounded. Lt van Maris reported that 'Cab' was shot at the foot of a flight of stairs leading to the upper floors as he covered the rest of the Section's retreat. Jack Coates says that he was killed inside the entrance archway to the courtyard as he attempted to fight off the attacking SS troops. Cpl Jim Peers (the only Section Corporal at the Police Station and 'Cab's' right hand man), reported before his death in 1991 that 'Cab' had been shot by one of the young SS soldiers because he refused to hand over his wristlet watch after capture. Jim Peers told this story to his family soon after his return from Prison Camp in 1945, and has repeated the story many times throughout the remainder of his life. Whatever the true circumstances of their Sergeant's death the young NCOs of his Section were made to step over his body as they were led from the building in to captivity. Lt van Maris remembers that the SS Commander ordered that the body be left lying on the pavement for 5 days as a warning to the Dutch people of what happened to anyone who crossed the SS troops.

Lt Wilf Morley and Jock Keddie were unaware of the events at the Police Station on that September afternoon. Both were still at Brigade HQ in the shadow of the bridge helping to guard the ever increasing number of prisoners as well as taking their place in the firing line as the Paras hung on with dogged determination. The enemy contented himself with constant heavy mortaring and shelling of the buildings which the British still occupied. A 68 ton King Tiger tank moved slowly through the streets in the early evening, pumping shell after shell into each house in turn bringing walls crashing down. The defenders simply knocked their way through into the house next door and carried on the fight from there. The Germans offered the British the opportunity to surrender, but Colonel Frost politely declined their offer and the savage fighting continued.

By Wednesday the 20th, 30 Corps were already 18 hours overdue. Ammunition at the bridge was down to a few rounds per gun. Food, water and medical stores were in desperately short supply and the men had just endured their third consecutive night without sleep, save what they could snatch between the fighting. Only the tenacity, determination and courage they had displayed in North Africa and Sicily kept the Paras hanging on. One by one the buildings around the bridge held by the men of the 1st Parachute Brigade were either reduced to a heap of smouldering rubble or turned into a raging inferno as the tanks fired their phosphorous shells through the shattered windows.

Colonel Frost was seriously wounded during the day and stretcher bearers carried him gently into the cellar of the Brigade HQ. The two exhausted RAMC Doctors were tending to the needs of over 200 seriously wounded who were crammed into the tiny underground rooms. The pungent smoke from the fires in the building above drifted down the steps into the cellars and it was obvious something drastic would have to be done if the wounded were not to be burnt alive. Amazingly, the Germans agreed to a two hour truce and the wounded men were carried from the cellars to be taken into captivity. When the last of the wounded had been driven away by the enemy in captured British Jeeps the fighting commenced again, but not before the German infantry had taken advantage of the truce to infiltrate three Companies of Panzer Grenadiers into British lines.

As the light faded on Wednesday evening there remained only about 140 Paratroopers still capable of fighting. The last of the food and water had gone and some of the rifles were down to their last clip of ammunition. This gallant band made their final stand amid the debris and destruction on the once proud Dutch houses beside

No 1 Section (1st Parachute Brigade)

the Rhine. Some tried to dodge their way back towards Oosterbeek where they knew the rest of the Division was holding out. Very few made it. Others decided to hide beneath the floorboards in unburnt houses, in the cellars, lofts or inside empty water tanks and to await the arrival of the 2nd Army.

By dawn on Thursday the 21st it was all over and Lt. Morley, Jock Keddie and the remaining defiant defenders were marched into captivity. But that wasn't to be the end of the drama as far as Lt Morley was concerned. Two days later on Saturday afternoon he was with a group of about 25 prisoners being taken by lorry from Velp to an interrogation centre at Zuphen, about 30 km north of Arnhem. As the vehicle slowly passed through the village of Brummen two of the prisoners, Majors Hibbert and Mumford leapt out and raced off between the houses. One of the SS guards fired after the fleeing prisoners but only succeeded in puncturing one of the vehicle's tyres and killing one of his fellow guards. He then ran to the rear of the lorry and emptied his Schmeiser into the crowd of prisoners, killing and wounding several of them. A local Dutch Doctor attempted to take care of the wounded but was roughly kicked away by the SS soldiers. Wilf Morley gave evidence to a War Crimes Commission following his release from Prison Camp after the war.

> Lieut F. L. Horton
> 1 Airborne Div. Provost Coy.
> A. P. D
> England
> 1·10·44
>
> Dear Mrs Whitnall,
>
> It is with deep regret that I write to inform you that your husband was not amongst those of the Company who returned from Arnhem.
>
> Information is scanty & it is impossible to say yet what has happened to your husband, who will be posted as missing believed prisoner of war.
>
> The sympathy of the whole Company is with you in the worry & uncertainty this news will bring, but I assure you that there is every hope of your husband being fit & well.
>
> Any further information will be forwarded to you as soon as possible but until your husband's location is definitely known, the following address should be used in corresponding with him.
>
> No. Rank Name.
> c/o Consul General,
> International Red Cross.
> Geneva,
> Switzerland.
>
> No unit must be used in this address.
>
> I sincerely hope to give you good news in the near future.
>
> I am.
> Yours Sincerely.
> F. L. Horton Lieut.

"A difficult task for the company officers after the evacuation"

CHAPTER 5

NUMBER 2 SECTION (ATT. 4TH PARACHUTE BRIGADE)

You could feel Gerry closing in, but you couldn't see him.
(Lcpl. 'Junior' Stubbs)

The shortage of aircraft available to the Division meant that the 4th Brigade were to be brought in with the 2nd Lift on D+1, Monday 18th September. The Brigade was made up of the 10th, 11th and 156th Parachute Battalions, plus Artillery, Medical, Engineer and other Support troops. The Brigade's objective was to occupy and defend the northern sector of the proposed defensive ring around Arnhem, and to await the arrival of the 2nd Army racing up from the south.

Attached to the 4th Brigade was Number 2 Section under Lieutenant F.R. de R. Locke of the Parachute Regiment. The Section personnel were Sgt. Austin Roberts, Cpls Jock Mills and Len Formoy and Lcpls Baker, Bazeley, Cardinelli, Harris, Fodd, Inns, Killen, Lawton, Purvey, Raine, Stubbs, Teece and Whiffen.

Lt Locke and three Provost NCOs, together with ten members of the Brigade Defence Platoon, were to fly in with the 1st Lift on the 17th and act as a reception party for the Brigade's glider transport due to arrive the following day. The Brigade Operation Order gave their tasks as:

> To mark the glider transport Landing Zone RV with Blue smoke.
> To receive, protect and marshal all Brigade gliderborne transport.

> To conduct all Brigade gliderborne transport to the Dispersal point and report arrival at the DP to the Officer Commanding 11th Battalion.

In addition they were to mark the Dropping Zone RV for the main groups arriving the following day, to establish wireless communications and to gather whatever information they could on the local situation.

One of the three NCO's to land with the Advance Party was 28 year old Lcpl Bill 'Stinger' Inns. The war had already taken him to the Orkney Islands, North Africa, Sicily, (where he narrowly escaped capture), and in to Italy with the Division. He remembers the flight in to Arnhem on the Sunday particularly because it was such a calm and uneventful trip on such a beautiful sunny day.

> *Very soon we arrived over the DZ. Lt. Locke was the first one out of the aircraft and I followed him out that fast that I was nearly standing on his 'chute. I remember doing a perfect landing right on the edge of the DZ, no rolling or anything. I just stood up, Knocked the box and my 'chute fell away. I was surprised to see a young Dutch girl running towards me and asking if she could have my parachute. I said that she could take it and then she said something to the effect that ... "We didn't expect you until Tuesday" ... That remark came as a bit of a bombshell. The group of us walked across the DZ towards our RV at the corner of a wood as the 1st Brigade sorted themselves out all around us. It was such a glorious day and we appeared to have caught the enemy completely by surprise. It was just like being on exercise in England.*
>
> *The rest of that first day was quite uneventful for our small party. We did a bit of patrolling around the area but we couldn't go too far as we were waiting for the rest of the 4th Brigade coming in the following day. I spent most of that first night lying behind a machine gun at the edge of a wood.*

At the exact time the Brigade were due to land on the following morning the area was attacked by around 30 Messerschmitts. It was as though the Germans knew the timings for the 2nd Lift. Fortunately the Brigade had been delayed on their UK airfields by bad weather and arrived over Holland some five hours late. By now the enemy were fully aware of the Allied landings and the incoming 4th Brigade aircraft received a far warmer reception than the 1st Lift on the previous day. Although heavily escorted by fighter planes, many of the aircraft were hit and a number were seen plunging towards the ground on fire. Bill Inns again:

> *That Monday morning we heard aircraft coming in low. We all thought that they were Spitfires coming in to clear the DZ, but they turned out to be Gerry planes. They started firing and the bullets were snapping off the little trees round us like carrots. I thought a plane could move fast, but you should have seen **us** move as we ran for better cover.*
>
> *We were getting a bit worried as time went by and there was no sign of the Brigade arriving. Then eventually the sky was filled with those lovely Dakotas and what a sight it was to see those thousands of Paras floating down to earth, and the gliders swooping down to land until the whole area was a mass of movement. We put the Blue smoke up to signify the RV and the transport started heading in our direction. We directed the drivers to their right locations and it was whilst I was talking to an Officer standing beside a vehicle that I took off my helmet and rested it, with my Sten, on the back of a vehicle and the driver drove off with my kit in the back. I never saw it again. I finished directing the transport then found myself a nice James motorcycle on the LZ. I leapt on and set off to find Brigade HQ and the rest of the Section.*

Lance Corporal 'Yoxy' baker had been a Regular Soldier for 10 years already at the time of Arnhem, being one of the first to volunteer for parachute training. He flew in with Number 2 Section on the 2nd Lift from Cottesmore.

> *We met a lot of flak on the way in, but what a sight at the DZ. Thousands of blokes, hundreds of gliders and the ground littered with vehicles and discarded parachutes. There were a number of fires burning and machine guns chattering away from the cover of some trees. We captured some very non-*

descript, scared Germans, but we took a fair number of casualties. I saw Lcpl Whiffen amongst them at the casualty station.

'Junior' Stubbs was also due to arrive that day. He had watched with awe as the armada of aircraft had passed overhead with the 1st Lift.

The news on the Sunday night was that there had been hardly any Ack-Ack fire at the planes and no opposition on the ground, so we thought we were in for a cushy time. We had an early start the next morning and I remember that a lot of locals were in tears as we left. We hung around at Brigade HQ for a while before the transport arrived to take us to the airfield. This is what I personally was jumping with:

The Section Bren gun plus spare barrel	
Six magazines for the Bren	
Riding gloves and goggles for Motor Cycle	
Signboards for marking Brigade HQ	
Full web equipment	
Two hand grenades	*Escape Kit*
Pistol and ammunition	*Respirator*
3 Shell dressings	*Gas Cape*
Steel helmet	*2 Water Bottles*
Toggle rope	*2 Ration Packs*
Torch	*Money*
Spare clothing	*Matches*
2 boxes Hexomides	*3 Hankies*
Writing material	*Gym shoes*
3 Pair of Socks	

Most of the bulky kit, including the Bren, haversacks, respirator, etc, all went in to my kitbag to be strapped to my leg when jumping. When I got my 'chute on, on top of all that lot, it was all I could do to move about. While we were waiting at the airfield we were given rations of meat sandwiches and tea. I put the sandwiches in my pocket to eat later. We clambered aboard the aircraft about 11.30 that morning and took off soon afterwards. We flew around for a time getting in to formation before heading off for the coast and Holland. There were rescue boats down below to pick up anyone unlucky enough to ditch in the sea, but we had lifejackets on under our parachute harness just in case.

When we reached the coast of Holland we saw that a lot of the land had been flooded. Despite our fighter escorts we were fired on quite a lot by light Ack-Ack and small arms fire. It sounded like a woodpecker tapping on the floor of the plane. Inside someone started up a bit of a sing-song to take our minds off things. An Officer passed round a tot of whisky each and then we were given the 20 minute warning. I strapped on my leg kitbag and had a thorough check of all my equipment. At 5 minutes the Red light came on and we all stood in line facing the exit. I looked out and saw hundreds of 'chutes on the ground so I knew that we had arrived. Bullets were hitting the aircraft and one of our American crewmen was firing his revolver through the open doorway. It probably relieved his tension a bit. Then the Green light was on and the chaps in front of me were leaping out. I struggled to the door with my bulky kitbag. Out went my leg, followed by the kitbag, followed by me. The 'chute opened quickly because of the extra weight I was carrying and I reached for the quick release which would allow the kitbag to drop on the end of a rope beneath me. But, the strap holding the quick release had slipped down to my ankle and I was unable to reach it. With my kitbag still attached to my leg I was in danger of a few broken bones when I hit the deck. I managed to manoeuvre my parachute so that I met Mother Earth in the following order; first the backs of my feet, then my backside, then the back of my head. It was a heavy landing and I was out cold for a few seconds. I carefully felt around for any broken bones, but luckily there weren't any. I just had a humdinger of a headache and a lack of skin on the shin of the leg carrying the kitbag. I struggled to get the Bren out of the kitbag and ready for action, then set off towards the Blue smoke that denoted Brigade HQ.

The DZ was under constant fire from mortars and small arms and we had taken a lot of casualties. At Brigade HQ I was given an area to cover with the Bren so I lay behind the gun and ate my meat sandwiches.

Number 2 Section gradually gathered at Brigade HQ as the NCOs arrived from around the DZ. The Brigade had landed on Ginkel Heath, between the Arnhem/Ede road and the main railway into Arnhem from the west, and about 8 miles from where the 2nd Battalion were fighting to retain a hold on the north end of the road bridge. The Brigade Commander, Brigadier J.W. Hackett, was quickly made aware of the events of the previous 24 hours and the fact that the 1st Brigade's push towards the bridge had been checked. The 11th Battalion, together with 2nd Battalion of the South Staffs from the Airlanding Brigade, were detached to 1st Brigade with orders to set off immediately towards Arnhem and the bridge.

The Provost Section, Brigade HQ Defence Platoon and other Brigade HQ personnel were quickly organising the defence of the Headquarters, interrupted by the occasional skirmish with disorganised groups of enemy. Sullen and dispirited prisoners were brought to the HQ along with captured enemy vehicles and weapons. Guarding the prisoners before they could be passed back to Div. HQ became another responsibility for the Provost Section. By 5pm, 2 hours after landing, the Section were reunited with Lt. Locke and the three NCOs who had arrived the previous day.

Protecting Ginkel Heath DZ as the Brigade landed was 1st Battalion KOSB from the Airlanding Brigade. A Dutch SS Battalion had been attempting to clear the KOSB from the woods bordering the DZ when the 2,000 men of the 4th Brigade dropped from the sky. The SS Commander, SS Captain Helle, was asleep at the time in his HQ, the Zuid-Ginkel Restaurant on the Arnhem/Ede road overlooking the heath. His SS Battalion were forced to beat a rapid retreat through the overwhelming weight of numbers against them.

Thirty year old John 'Jock' Mills was one of the two Provost Section Corporals who dropped on Ginkel Heath that day. The war had already seen him plucked from the Mole at Dunkirk and fighting his way across North Africa with the 6th Armoured Div.

before volunteering for airborne duties. He remembers that day very well:

> *After we landed we gathered the Section together and made for a large house nearby. It must have been some sort of Café or Restaurant because the owner had just got a meal ready for some German Officers. There was a bit of shooting before we chased the Germans out and finished off their meal. The owner of the place was overjoyed to see us and gave us some more food. Looking at one of the dead Germans on the floor I realised that we wouldn't be facing second-rate troops as we had been led to believe. He had the 'Lightening Flashes' of the SS on his collar and I knew we would be in for a hard time.*

The intelligence information available before Market-Garden was put into operation had led the planners to firmly believe that the Division would be met by only light opposition. It was anticipated that the Germans, already reeling and on the run from the Normandy landings the previous June, would not offer much resistance, and that the troops billeted in and around Arnhem would be of inferior quality. The total enemy strength was expected to be ... 'around 3,000 men with a few guns and tanks' ... and mainly of the 'Home Guard' and Hitler Youth type. Not surprisingly the consensus of opinion throughout the Division was that it would be a 'walk-over'.

The facts were somewhat different. Two Panzer Divisions had recently arrived in the Arnhem area to reinforce and replenish their armour and weapons. An SS Panzer Grenadier Training Battalion, together with an SS NCOs School were undergoing training in the woods outside the town, and the Dutch SS Battalion, which was soon to attack the KOSB, was billeted at Ede to the west. By midnight on the 17th an additional 10 Battalions had been hastily assembled in Arnhem having been rushed there in whatever transport was available; farm carts, cycles, requisitioned civilian cars and wood burning lorries, even old Fire Engines. German soldiers on leave in the German villages and towns just over the nearby border were rounded up to join the fighting. Ad hoc infantry units were formed from SS veterans, navy, airforce, administrative and office staff and Military Police. By dawn on the 18th a further 6 Battalions had been formed to the west and were advancing on a 6km front towards the Drop and Landing Zones.

The enemy were experts at assembling improvised units at short notice to exploit a weakness in the Airborne Division's defences or to counter a particular threat. Hardly surprising then, that the 2nd Lift on the 18th had received such a hostile reception and that the 4th Brigade's original plans had been thrown in to such total confusion. This book will not attempt to record in detail the complex movements and actions of the 4th Brigade, or indeed the rest of the Division, as that has been most adequately recorded in a number of excellent accounts over the years. We will simply confine our story to the activities of the Provost Section involved in the confusion of the battle, and to individual recollections of events at the time.

Throughout the 18th and 19th of September Brigade HQ and Number 2 Section were constantly moving location as the rapidly fluctuating battle situation dictated. Their action was concentrated either side of the railway line between Ginkel Heath and the village of Wolfheze with it's important railway level crossing. The Brigade Commander was still intent on the Brigade fighting its way through to Arnhem, as was the original plan, but the enemy opposition blocking his route was stiffening by the hour.

Enemy prisoners being brought to Brigade HQ were causing something of an embarrassment and were dispatched under escort to Div. HQ. Lcpl 'Claude' Raine was one of the escorts.

> *At Arnhem I kept on doing things which an old soldier never does, I kept volunteering. When a patrol was sent out from Brigade to try and reach Div. HQ. I volunteered to go with Cpl. Mills and escort some prisoners back. But, the patrol had wheels and **we** were on foot so that in a matter of minutes we were on our own with the prisoners. We came to a clearing in the wood and a large house nearby. Cpl. Mills said that he would go and get some water and left me guarding the prisoners. While he was away there was heavy firing coming*

from the direction we were heading and the patrol came racing back telling us to get the hell out of it because they were being chased by tanks. I waited for Cpl. Mills to come back then we took the prisoners back to Brigade HQ. The Brigade Commander saw us coming back in and said ... "Well done lads". That made us feel very proud.

Corporal 'Jock' Mills remembers the confusion at the time:

*I spent a lot of time in the woods digging holes. I suppose we were fighting a rearguard action, but for all **we** knew we could have been **advancing**. We didn't know **what** was going on. Did we?*

I remember on one occasion I was with some members of the Section sheltering in a trench from a particular heavy mortar attack. We were well below ground level and didn't see this Officer approaching. He asked who we were and what we were doing. I told him that we were guarding Brigade HQ. He said that the HQ had .... off and that he was ....ing off too and that we had better .... off because the ....ing Germans were coming. I looked over the top of the trench and they were too. We .... off as well.

On one occasion we had taken some prisoners back to Div. HQ and were guarding them before they were put in to the cage at the tennis courts. An RAMC Officer said that a lot of wounded, who were having to lie out in the open, were being wounded again by enemy mortar rounds hitting the tree tops and 'airbursting'. He said that he needed some trenches for the wounded to shelter in. I got another couple of out lads and we motioned to the German prisoners to get digging. They were frightened at first and refused, thinking that we were making them did their own graves. Once they realised the trenches were for the wounded they were OK.

Many of the Provost NCOs had previous infantry experience before transferring to the CMP. Lcpl. Bert 'Junior' Stubbs had served with the Lincolnshire Regiment and was 'entrusted' with the Section Bren gun. 'Jock' Mills again:

> *We were in the woods, I've no idea where, and I was hit in the arm by a sniper. He was lying behind a fallen tree and I pointed him out to 'Junior' who fired a burst from the Bren. He hit the sniper first time but kept on firing because every time he hit him the body jumped from the impact and 'Junior' thought he was jumping to avoid the fire. I had to knock the Bren down otherwise 'Junior' would have used up a full mag of valuable ammunition.*

The Section became depleted in numbers during those first two or three days. Lcpl Whiffen had been wounded on the DZ and had played no further part, others were detailed to escort prisoners back to Div.HQ only to find that the enemy had cut off their route back to the Brigade. They then joined forces with the Div. HQ Provost Section, by now at the Hartenstein Hotel, and took their place in the defence of the Headquarters.

The 4th Brigade was under almost incessant attack from small arms fire, mortars, self-propelled guns and even tanks. Small groups of paratroopers would find themselves cut off and fighting their own bloody battle. Enemy tanks would be stalked through the woods or narrow lanes and knocked out in individual acts of magnificent bravery. Attacks also came from the air as enemy fighter planes raked the woods with cannon fire. 'Stinger' Inns was at Brigade HQ when it came under attack from a group of ME 109s:

> *We were dug in around the HQ, very sandy soil but just a tangle of fallen tree trunks and roots when you tried to dig in. Some supplies were dropped nearby by the RAF but they landed high up in the trees and we couldn't reach them. Then these Gerry planes came over and started strafing us. The shells were tearing in to the ground all around us so I made a run for a brick building with a haystack next to it. Then they set the bloody haystack on fire so I had to make a run for cover under a little bridge.*

Lcpl 'Yoxy' Baker was one of those to become separated from the Section soon after leaving the DZ. Following the railway line in the direction of Arnhem the group he was with ran in to opposition and he lost contact with the rest of the Section. He joined up with a group of Glider Pilots and fought his way through to Div. HQ at the Hartenstein where he reported to the Provost RSM for duty.

The hazardous events aren't the only ones remembered by those who took part and the British soldier will always find humour in adversity. 'Claude' Raine was dug in close to Brigade HQ by the railway line and sharing a trench with his mate, Lcpl Jack Purvey. Jack needed to attend to an urgent call of nature and was literally caught with his trousers down when the area was strafed by enemy aircraft. When the dust and the smoke cleared he could be seen upside down in the trench minus his trousers.

It must have been around the same time, when the Section were dug in along the railway embankment west of Wolfheze, that Bill Inns came face to face with the enemy for the first time. He had not managed to replace his Sten which disappeared on the back of a truck, but he still had his James motor cycle. He explains:

It was a hot day and the lads said that they had no water left. I collected what water bottles I could and set off for the Railway Station at Wolfheze to find a tap. The Station was still in our hands so I knew that it would be OK. On the second or third trip with the water bottles I saw a couple of Germans on the path in front of me. I stopped the bike, drew my pistol and shouted ... "Hande Hoch" ... They surrendered right away so I took them back to Brigade HQ. I set off again for the Station with another load of water bottles, riding along this narrow, dusty track and throwing up a huge cloud of dust behind me. Not far from the Station a German plane appeared and started machine gunning the path in front of me. I crashed the bike and dived behind a tree for cover and watched the plane as it flew off. I was just about to make a dash for the Station when a Spandau machine gun opened up on me as I hid behind the tree. I was still carrying three bandoliers of .303 ammunition and a Sten waistcoat which held about 8 full magazines, but all I had to defend myself with was my little .38 revolver. I was firing in the direction of the Spandau, but you could hardly hear the revolver for the din going on. I turned sideways behind the narrow tree to try and get a bit more cover and that's when I noticed that my clothing was on fire. I don't know if the Spandau was using tracer as well. Anyway, I had a bit of a panic as I set about beating out the flames. I was still letting off the odd shot with my revolver when it suddenly went very quiet. What followed was the weirdest experience that I have ever had. I was up in the air, about 50 feet looking down on myself. I could see everything that was going on down below. I could see some of our lads behind the trees, I could see the Spandau in a shell hole firing in my direction and other enemy soldiers crouching behind trees who I shouldn't have been able to see at all. I was looking down on all this from a great height as though I wasn't part of it. And then it was all over. The deafening noise started again and I was down behind my little tree.

The first thing I felt was a searing pain in my left thigh, like a red hot poker being pushed in to me. I tried to make myself small and get a little more cover behind the tree, but I was too wide and the tree was too narrow. When I tried to reload my .38 I found that I couldn't bend my left elbow and there was blood running down onto my hand. I realised that I had been shot through the elbow too. That's when I decided that I had better surrender. I slung the revolver away, put my one good arm in the air and stepped from behind the tree.

No 2 Section (4th Parachute Brigade)

Duty Order for a Corporal of the Divisional Provost Company in Italy.

Land Army Girls at Stubton Rectory 1943/4. L/R rear Ruby, Elsie, Beryl, Hilda (now Mrs Harry Wilce), Emmie, Joan, Marjorie, "Red", Doris. L/R centre Lily, Ena, Audrey, Babs, Joyce, Dorothy, Dot, Helen. L/R front Edna, Vera, Cathy, Edna, Marjorie, Doris ("Half-Pint") Mrs Jock Wright, Beryl.

No 2 Section (4th Parachute Brigade)

A Group of Military Policeman board one of the main Dakotas bound for Arnhem. Fifth in line is Jock Keddie standing in front of the bare-headed Mick Cox. Eighth from the steps is Jock Wright

Kitted up just before Arnhem. L/R Lcpls Wright, Phillips and Plummell.

No 2 Section (4th Parachute Brigade)

The main Arnhem Police Station in 1950. The entrance to the courtyard can be seen on the extreme right.

One of the female German prisoners at Arnhem.

German POW's inside the Hartenstein tennis courts with Sgt Yardley, RSM Kibble and Captain Gray.

No 2 Section (4th Parachute Brigade)

A group of SS prisoners closely guarded by Glider Pilots.

Defending Div. HQ at the Hartenstein Hotel.

No 2 Section (4th Parachute Brigade)

'Junior' Stubbs watched Bill Inns ride off on his motor bike. He was dug in along the railway line with Lcpl Fred Cardinelli, his Number 2 on the Bren. They had both been at Brigade HQ when it had come under attack from the ME109s, and had both come through the experience unscathed. Now they were lying behind the Bren peering along the railway line in the direction of the unseen enemy.

We watched the Polish gliders coming in during the afternoon and landing just to our left, then the supply planes dropping much needed weapons, ammunition and medical supplies. The sight that followed was enough to make you weep. We watched the German Ack-Ack knocking the planes out of the sky. Planes were coming down in flames and the men inside them still pushing the supplies out of the door instead of saving their own lives. The sad thing was, we were surrounded and nearly all the supplies were falling amongst the Germans. Smoke from crashed planes was rising skywards wherever you looked. I think I can honestly say it was the worst sight I have ever seen.

Some of the Poles managed to join up with us, but there was much confusion caused by the Poles firing on some of our lads, and us firing back. There were times when we didn't know who was who. Things were really hotting up and Gerry was within about a quarter of a mile of us. They had captured the Wolfheze Railway Station and were firing along the railway lines at us. While this was going on our Battalions were being withdrawn from the woods into a better defensive position and in no time at all we found ourselves as the main line of defence. An Officer appeared in a Bren Carrier and ordered us to get out so we scrambled out of our hole and down the embankment under fire. The Bren Carrier covered us and we dashed through a tunnel underneath the railway.

We piled into some Jeeps and tried to make a dash through the enemy lines, but it was no good so we turned back. The Brigadier said that we would spend the night there with the men we had available. Brigade HQ was about 200 strong by this time and made up of men from the KOSB, 156th Battalion, then odds and sods like ourselves, Police, Defence Platoon, Engineers, etc. We dug in along the embankment and in the woods and waited. That night was one of the worst I've spent. You could feel Gerry closing in around us, but you couldn't see him. Firing broke out now and then just to keep us on our toes and make sure nobody got any sleep.

On the night 19/20 September the Divisional Commander decided to withdraw the 4th Brigade into the rapidly forming defence Perimeter around the Hartenstein Hotel at Oosterbeek, about 4 miles west of Arnhem. What remained of the Brigade, about 270 members of the 156th Battalion, 250 of the 10th Battalion, together with the Brigade HQ Group, set off at first light on the 20th to fight their way through to Div.HQ.

Throughout the day the Brigade fought a series of obstinate rearguard actions to disengage itself from the enemy and establish a defensive line at Oosterbeek. By the end of that day they had lost many gallant men killed and wounded. In addition, the enemy had captured 800 members of the Brigade, together with a quantity of irreplaceable mortars, anti-tank guns and vehicles. 'Junior' Stubbs again:

First thing on Wednesday morning we piled into the few available Jeeps to try another breakthrough. We drove slowly through the woods, weapons at the ready and eyes peeled in case Gerry showed himself. We stopped just off the main road to Arnhem, close to Oosterbeek, and an Officer went off on the back of a motor bike to see if everything was OK. We heard some machine gun fire and the Officer came staggering back followed by the Dispatch Rider. They had both been badly shot up by a tank about 200 yards down the road. A Royal Artillery Officer told me to follow him with the Bren to see if we could get close to the tank. We crawled to within about 75 yards of the tank and I thought that I could put my shots through the tank's observation slits. I never got the chance because the Jeeps started heading off back in to the woods without us both, so we made a dash for them and just about managed to get in to the last one.

The Brigadier tried another route to get round the tank but wherever we went through the woods we seemed to be under a constant hail of small arms fire from all sides. At one point we dug in along the side of a road and I set up the Bren in a small dug-out and fired at anything that moved. An enemy troop carrier came slowly out of the wood further down the road and 'Robbo' our Section Sergeant, collared the Bren and opened fire at it with me lying in the road changing empty magazines for him. The carrier didn't get very far and 'Robbo' felt better for letting off steam.

By now we were being shelled and mortared incessantly and some of the Jeeps were on fire and I remember Sergeant Roberts leaping into one of them and driving it clear of the rest of the jeeps. I was still having pot shots at anything that crossed the road in front of me, and I certainly got a few of them. We had taken some prisoners and we made them do the digging for us. We let them dig their own holes in front of ours. I think a lot of them were killed by their own side.

Later that same day I was with Fred Cardinelli and Jack Lawton when a gun opened up on us from about 100 yards away. I think it was a depressed Ack-Ack gun and it was causing a heck of a lot of casualties. I fired off a magazine at the gun and must have hit some of the crew because the gun went silent. I was then given instructions to lay a belt of fire just ahead of some of our chaps who were going to try and get through the woods. I fired just in front of them until my ammunition ran out. That was it, there was no more .303 ammunition available. I buried the bolt from the Bren to make sure Gerry couldn't use it, then slung the rest of the weapon away.

The group I was with, less than 100 of us, were nearly all out of ammunition, I think about 75% were wounded, and we were totally surrounded. Tanks and heavy guns were firing at us from almost point blank range, setting the few remaining Jeeps on fire and snapping off the trees and branches above our heads. Without ammunition there

> *wasn't a lot we could do. I think someone took the lead and shoved up a white flag, then they were on us from all directions, hundreds of them. Mostly SS and some 17 or 18 year old youths. The older Germans were OK but the youths were pigs. The one who searched me wouldn't even let me keep my water bottle. Any bits of food we had we were made to dump. They formed us up on the road ready to march away. A Gerry SS Officer came round and patted some of the Paras on the shoulder and said ... "Good fight Tommy".*

Sergeant Austin Roberts and a number of the Section NCOs remained as close as possible to Brigade HQ throughout the day. All Security Duties forgotten now and they were fighting for survival as out and out infantry soldiers. Sgt. Roberts had received a couple of shrapnel wounds already that day but continued to be a constant inspiration to the young NCO's around him. The accounts of his death are contradictory from the few sources available, but the most reliable would suggest that the following are the most likely sequence of events.

Sometime during the 19th, 'Robbo' had acquired a Bren because he was seen that day at Brigade HQ collecting ammunition. One of the shrapnel wounds he received was probably quite severe as Lcpl 'Claude' Raine speaks of seeing him with his sleeve in tatters and bleeding profusely. On the 19th Cpl Jock Mills was with 'Robbo' in the woods beside the Valkenburglaan, just north of the Koude Herberg on Utrechseweg. He remembers:

> *There was fierce fighting taking place when we heard the sound of tank engines. Sergeant Roberts thought that they were **our** tanks coming to relieve us. I knew that they were enemy tanks and I tried to warn 'Robbo' to take cover but, as he began running towards the sound of the engines, a German tank burst through the undergrowth and sprayed the area with machine gun fire. 'Robbo' was hit several times and killed instantly. The tank drove into the clearing, still firing, but the gunner couldn't depress his gun low enough to hit me. I jumped into a shell hole then, as the tank turned away, I ran deeper in to the wood.*

What was left of the Provost Section was overrun at the same time that 'Junior' Stubbs was captured. That is, on the afternoon of the 20th September as the decimated 4th Brigade fought its way from Wolfheze towards Div. HQ at the Hartenstein. The Section had remained alongside Brigade HQ throughout the previous 48 hours of almost constant attack by aircraft, tanks, self-propelled guns, mortars and a storm of small arms fire. They had seen their lightly-armed comrades practically defenceless against the overwhelming firepower of the enemy, and stared in frustration as much-needed supplies fell from the sky into the waiting arms of the Germans.

Now they crouched beneath the Brigade's Jeeps drawn up under the trees. One by one the vehicles erupted in a hail of flying metal as a tank shell found its mark. Shards of red-hot metal tore into flesh leaving another paratrooper in agony on the ground. Cpl. Mills still remembers the moment of capture with some anguish after all these years:

> We had no ammo left and we could see the enemy moving in towards us. I'd told the lads to get rid of the bolts out of their weapons. I crawled under a bush to try and hide but the next thing I felt was a kick up the backside. I looked round and saw the biggest German I had ever seen. I was dragged out, frisked for weapons and pushed out into the road. At first I couldn't understand why they were congratulating us for fighting so well, they were even giving us cigarettes and water. Some of us thought that we would be shot after Hitler saying that all Paras were terrorists who had to be shot at once. We were treated quite well by the SS who had captured us.
>
> We were being marched down the road in a long column, all of us who had been captured in the wood. From somewhere up ahead a German opened up on us with a machine gun or something. We all dived in to a ditch for cover. When the German Officer ordered us out onto the road again we refused as long as we were being fired at. The Officer said, ... "He will not fire at you any more" ... With that he walked down the road, up to the German soldier who had fired at us, shouted at him, then shot him dead. I felt

> *sorry for the soldier because there was still a lot of fighting going on in the area and he had obviously made a mistake. But it shows that the German military had a strict code of honour.*

'Junior' Stubbs who, as far as we know, has not met 'Jock' Mills since the end of the war, tells a similar account of their capture.

> *They marched us a couple of hundred yards down to a main road where there were German tanks lined up as far as we could see. This German, a marine I think he was, started firing at us as we marched towards him. Lieutenant Locke was hit in the arm or shoulder and Len Formoy took a bullet through his cheek. In one cheek and out the other side. He said it was a good job he had his false teeth out at the time. The German was shot dead by one of our guards. 'Locky' and Formoy were taken away by a German ambulance and we never saw them again.*

The original Number 2 Section, who only a few days previously had been kicking their heels in Lincolnshire, was now no more. The Section Sergeant who had trained and guided them over the past two years was lying dead in the wood behind them. Lieutenant Locke, who had paid for their drinks on the night before they left England, was badly wounded and on his way to hospital along with Len Formoy and two or three of the Lance Corporals. Two other members, Lcpls Bazeley and Baker, were somewhere at Div. HQ defending the Perimeter but were later to make it safely back to Allied lines south of the river. The rest of the Section were being marched away in to captivity.

As Lcpl Raine was to remark some years later:

> *Arnhem for me seemed to have three phases. A glorious send off as we left England on the Monday. We had a marvellous return from prison Camp the following April, but the bit in between was not so good.*

CHAPTER 6

NUMBER 3 SECTION (ATT. AIRLANDING BRIGADE)

I thought, Hell, they're giving themselves up, and we're pulling out.

(Lcpl Dennis Fitzgerald)

The 1st Airlanding Brigade comprised 3 Battalions, the 1st Battalion of the Border Regiment, the 2nd Battalion South Staffordshire Regiment and the 7th Battalion King's Own Scottish Borderers, (KOSB), together with support troops and a Field Ambulance Unit. Number 3 Section of the Div. Provost Company had also been attached since the Brigade was formed.

Prior to operation Market-Garden the Section Sergeant, one of the Section Corporals and three of the Lance Corporals were detached to travel with the Seaborne Element in the August. The reduced Section which landed at Arnhem was under the command of Lieutenant Frank Horton of the South Staffs, with Cpl. Jock Moir and Lcpls Chapman, Charles, Downton, Fitzgerald, Howells, McColl, Pawsey, Riley, Quinn, plus two additional Lcpls whose names are unknown. The Brigade Commander's report following the Operation stated that Provost strength on landing had been one Officer and twelve Other Ranks. The members of the Section were also fully trained paratroopers to enable the exchange of NCOs between Sections.

It may be pertinent here to explain the gliders used by the Brigade and their method of take-off and landing. The American

WACO, known as the HADRIAN to the British, had been used extensively in North Africa and Sicily. It could carry either a Jeep, a 6 Pounder anti-tank gun plus crew, or 15 fully equipped troops. The HORSA was much larger with a correspondingly greater carrying capacity of 28 fully equipped troops or a 6 Pounder anti-tank gun plus crew, towing Jeep and ammunition. The HAMILCAR was the largest of the three and was designed to carry heavy loads of 60 troops or a small tank.

The main type used was the HORSA, 67 feet long with a wing span of 88 feet, it was made almost entirely of wood and had a fixed undercarriage. This could be jettisoned if necessary and the landing made on a skid. The glider was loaded through a door on the port side just behind the pilot. For quick unloading in action the tail section could be removed by undoing a number of bolts and then slicing through the control wires with bolt cutters.

The glider was usually towed by Armstrong Whitleys, Albemarles, Halifaxes or Sterling aircraft. The second two were four engined bombers adapted for towing and were normally used to tow the much heavier HAMILCARS.

To get the HORSA into the air it was attached to the tow aircraft, from two strong points on the wings, by a nylon cable with a breaking point of several tons. The aircraft moved down the runway at full throttle, gradually taking up the slack on the cable. The HORSA would reach flying speed before the tow aircraft and the glider pilot then eased it into the air, keeping it flying slightly higher than the tug to lessen the strain on the tow aircraft's engines. Once both were airborne the glider pilot could fly either above or below the tow depending on weather conditions, and to try and avoid the turbulence from the aircraft's engine. The tow and glider pilots were in telephone contact via a cable running through the tow rope.

Once the glider pilot had pulled the lever to release the cable the glider was on its own. Those on board were relieved to be rid of the ear-shattering noise of the aircraft's engines up ahead of them, and the constant vibration of the glider in the aircraft's slipstream. For a few minutes, provided they were not on the receiving end of unfriendly fire, they could appreciate the relative quiet with the only sound being that of the wind rushing past, and the glider appearing to hang motionless in the air. The pilot, who held the rank of Sergeant or above in the Glider Pilot Regiment, then took over and needed all his skill and training to set the glider and its passengers safely down on the Landing Zone. He had to adopt a steep gliding angle to maintain flying speed, keep his eye on the LZ and gradually lose height in a series of descending turns. Once he had selected his landing 'spot', large flaps on the wings helped him to vary the glide angle and speed before he finally touched down with brakes full on and a brake-assisting parachute streaming out behind the glider.

But it didn't always work out so smoothly. Sutton Grimshaw was a Sgt. Glider Pilot. On the 17th September 1944 he was the pilot of HORSA glider Number 13 heading for Arnhem. He describes the approach and landing:

> We left Down Ampney for Arnhem with a load of 6 men plus a Jeep and trailer of ammunition. My 2nd Pilot was a Sergeant Brown. We ran into cloud over the North Sea but the 'angle of dangle' string hanging in front of me in the cockpit kept us on a level and even course. On my approach over the LZ I chose a spot to land and came in at about 80-90 miles an hour. There was a sudden loud bang from the rear of the glider and my speed shot up to about 120. In addition, another glider had chosen to land on the spot I was heading for. I saw a narrow gap between him and the trees and headed for it travelling far too fast. I landed at about 120 miles an hour and the left wing smacked into a thick tree. The glider spun round through 90 degrees and branches of the tree crashed through the nose of the glider battering me around the head and face. The 2nd Pilot, passengers and Jeep were all OK. I was left propped against a tree for about 4 or 5 hours before the Medics took me to a barn they were using as a Casualty Station.

The Airlanding Brigade, less half of the South Staffs, were to fly into Arnhem with the 1st Lift on the 17th and land at Reijers Camp. This was an area of open land between the trees across the railway line north of Wolfheze, and was designated LZ 'S'. The tasks of the brigade were:

1. To seize and hold the DZs and LZs
2. To cover the unloading of the 1st Lift
3. To protect the arrival of the 2nd Lift on the 18th
4. To protect the landing of the Polish gliders on the 3rd Lift

The Provost Section would carry out their normal role with Brigade HQ of guiding troops and vehicles to RV points from the LZ, security duties, guarding any prisoners, escorts and the defence of Brigade HQ together with the Defence Platoon. Within the Airlanding Brigade the Provost NCOs also appear to have had a closer liaison with the individual Battalions than was the case in the two Parachute Brigades.

The 160 gliders carrying the Brigade lifted off from Down Ampney, Blakehill, Fairford, Broadwell and a dozen other airfields around Brize Norton in Oxfordshire. There was a slight ground mist as the first of the gliders was lifted into the air just before 10am to circle the countryside before joining the colossal armada heading towards Holland. The Provost Section was, unusually, allocated one glider to carry the NCOs and the Section Jeep. It was normal practice to distribute such small units throughout a number of gliders in case one was brought down or failed to arrive at the destination. Cpl Jock Moir recalls the flight over:

> We went from Brize Norton that Sunday morning. I should have gone by aircraft but for some reason this was changed and I still had my 'chute with me in the glider. It was an uneventful trip over on a lovely sunny day. There was the odd bit of firing when we landed, but nothing to worry about. Our job was to lay down Blue markers on the LZ but we never got that far, the gliders were coming in too fast.

Lcpl Dennis Fitzgerald had joined the Northamptonshire Regiment in 1938 when he was just 17 and had volunteered for parachute training as soon as he heard about the new airborne forces. On the ship returning from North Africa in 1943 he met some members of the Div. Provost Company and transferred to CMP when the Division settled in Lincolnshire. He had been with Airlanding Brigade ever since.

No 3 Section (1st Airlanding Brigade)

The day we landed at Arnhem was just like an exercise. We'd had a pleasant flight over, the weather and the scenery were great, and when we landed I can't remember a shot being fired at us. It all seemed so easy. It was only later that all hell broke loose.

After some slight difficulty removing the tail section of the glider the Section Jeep was unloaded and Lt. Horton led the NCOs to join up with Brigade HQ at the RV. By 4pm on that Sunday afternoon HQ and Number 3 Section were established in a house in the northern outskirts of Wolfheze, close to the level crossing. The infantry battalions took up their positions guarding the LZs and DZs in readiness for the arrival of the 2nd Lift on the following day. Patrols from Brigade HQ, including the Provost NCOs, searched the surrounding houses rounding up odd pockets of enemy troops. The Brigade Commander's report says:

Some prisoners were taken during the evening, mostly from the artillery and SS transit personnel. A German WAAF was found by 7 KOSB in civilian clothing. She refused food until it had first been tasted by British troops.

Dennis Fitzgerald remembers the same female:

This German female was brought in late on the first day. I think she was Luftwaffe, dressed in white blouse, grey two-piece costume and very attractive with fair hair. Some time later 'Buck' Riley and I had to take her off to Div. HQ to be interrogated. We went in the Jeep but had to leave it after a while and set off to complete the journey on foot. She signalled that she had to 'spend a penny' so we motioned her to walk a few yards away to some bushes. It was dusk and the light was fading but there was a sudden brief glimpse of white thigh through the bushes and I remember averting my eyes. There we were, in the middle of a battle, playing the gentleman. We found our way to Div. HQ and dropped her off with the Intelligence. I saw her some time later when I was escorting more prisoners there. She wasn't in the Tennis

Courts Cage with all the other prisoners, but standing on the veranda outside the Hartenstein under guard. I seem to remember she was making something out of parachute silk.

Jock Moir also recalls the first of the prisoners captured by the Brigade:

Going down the road from the LZ towards the first Brigade HQ we picked up 9 or 10 German prisoners out of the various houses we searched. On the road we met some of our Engineers who asked if we had seen an ammunition dump on the way. We sent them to where we had seen the dump and I think it was their job to blow it up. We had the prisoners lying face down in the roadway all the time. They were a pretty scared looking lot.

That first night was relatively quiet for the Brigade with only a couple of skirmishes on the landing grounds. By morning the enemy activity increased considerably as the Germans reacted rapidly and violently to the landings of the previous day. Enemy aircraft strafed the woods and the landing grounds while the defending infantry waited for the arrival of the 2nd Lift. This was due to arrive at around 10am, precisely when the LZs and DZs were attacked from the air, but bad weather in England had delayed take-off and it was 5 hours later before the first of the paratroopers and gliders came in. The delay had resulted in the loss of many of the Airlanding Brigade who were dug in defending the landing areas.

Dennis Riley's job for the first couple of days was delivering messages between Brigade and Div. HQs on his motor cycle, finding his way along the maze of narrow roads and sandy tracks through the woods. Eventually he was stopped by a Private in the South Staffs who informed him that if he went any further he would run straight in to the enemy. Dennis returned to Brigade HQ, parked up his machine for the last time and found himself a place in one of the trenches.

On that same day, Monday the 18th, information came through that the Div. Commander, Major General Urquhart, was missing after he had followed 1st Brigade in to Arnhem. The Commander of the Airlanding Brigade, Brigadier 'Pip' Hicks was his nominated replacement and he set off for Div. HQ at the Hartenstein. Dennis Fitzgerald explains what happened next:

> *When the General went missing and Brigadier Hicks took command of the Division I took him down to the Hartenstein and spent the night there with him. I used one of the tablecloths from the hotel as a cover that night and tried to get some sleep. I think the Brigadier's original bodyguard, a Warrant Officer from the Army Physical Training Corps, had been killed or wounded and Pete Downton and I were detailed to take over and escort the Brigadier everywhere he went.*

Once the 2nd Lift was down the Brigade HQ moved location closer to Div. HQ and established itself in the sumptuous Bilderberg Hotel. As the Brigade Commander later reported:

> *This had the disadvantage of being an obvious artillery and mortar target, in the front line, and almost entirely composed of glass. But it was in the true tradition of the Airlanding Brigade as being the most luxurious building in the area. The Dutch proprietors were most hospitable to us and seem to have been the same to the Germans as they produced a number of chits signed by individual German Officers. It was decided to leave this HQ at dawn the following morning.*

Dennis Riley remembered that part of the operation for the comfortable bed he found in the Hotel. The only decent sleep he had the whole time there, but he couldn't get used to the strange bed cover. (Duvets had not reached England in 1944!) The Provost Section were again part of the defence and security for the HQ and dug in around the Hotel as the light faded on that September evening. About 7am the following morning, Tuesday the 19th, General Urquhart made his way back to Div. HQ and Brigadier Hicks returned to the Brigade. As the Brigadier had predicted, the magnificent Bilderberg Hotel soon attracted the enemy's attention and it was attacked by Messerschmitts during the morning. The HQ staff were already on the transport ready to move to a new location when the aircraft struck and fortunately suffered no casualties. The Headquarters and the Provost Section then moved to a group of houses close to the Div. HQ. Jock Moir recalls the time:

> *We dug in under the trees which was OK at first because they were full of leaves and gave us plenty of cover. In fact it was quite dark under there. After a while though all the leaves had been shot off with the shelling and you could see right through to the sky. What got through to the lads was the intensity of the shelling on those few days. We were pounded like hell and the power of the explosions seemed to lift up your whole stomach. You felt so helpless sitting there in the trench and not being able to fight back.*

Throughout the day Brigade HQ came under heavy mortar and shellfire as the defenders tried to make some sort of order out of the chaos. The Provost NCOs dug their slit trenches around the HQ houses, their role as Military Policemen virtually abandoned as they fought for their very survival alongside the other members of the Brigade. All the time the enemy's strength was increasing as ad hoc units were rushed into Oosterbeek and Arnhem, effectively splitting the British forces into two pockets, at the Hartenstein Hotel and the bridge. Tanks, self-propelled guns, heavy artillery and mortars were pounding the British positions almost at will. Fighting back with their light 6 Pounder anti-tank guns, PIATs, (Projector Infantry Anti-Tank), Gammon bombs, (which would stick to the hull of a tank if the paratrooper could get close enough to throw it), mortars and even hand grenades, the Paras were holding their ground. Individual acts of outstanding bravery became commonplace as tanks were stalked and destroyed, enemy gun positions single-handedly wiped out, or men risked their lives to bring in urgently needed supplies to their hard pressed comrades. And still the interminable shelling went on. Dennis Fitzgerald again:

> *I remember being in a trench with another MP close to Brigade HQ. We were being shelled by something big every*

few minutes and the shells were landing so close that the whole ground was shaking. It was like when you hit a cricket ball with the edge of the bat and you can feel the shock all up your arm, only this time it was your whole body that felt the shock.

The detailed planning of Market-Garden included a number of re-supply drops by the RAF of ammunition, weapons, food, medical supplies, etc, to be delivered to designated Dropping Points. The aircraft duly arrived, flying in at 1,000 feet through an intensive barrage of flak, to drop their much needed canisters. Unfortunately the areas were still in German hands and the battle weary Paras could only watch in despair as the supplies floated down to the enemy. Only a handful of the almost 400 tons of desperately needed supplies fell off target and were recovered by the British. A new Dropping Point had been hastily marked with yellow strips of cloth close to Div. HQ but had been immediately strafed by enemy aircraft. The area was also partially hidden by trees and was spotted by only a few of the supply pilots as they flew through the hail of flak towards the prearranged DP.

The British soldier's ingenuity under the most difficult conditions is legendary, particularly when it comes to providing himself with creature comforts and food. Brigade HQ being situated in a residential area meant that there was a ready supply of vegetables and fruit in many of the well kept gardens. Jock Moir remembers the carrots and cabbages dug up during a lull in the shelling and made in to a warming soup. If the men were lucky there was also the occasional tame rabbit left behind by the departing residents which found its way in to the pot. There was a report of a tame 'moggy' ending its days surrounded by various vegetables over a fire. The diners were convinced that it was rabbit as they enquired if here were any 'seconds'. In the interests of a few now elderly and delicate stomachs, we will refrain from revealing which Section was involved in that particular episode!

On Wednesday the 20th the Divisional Commander acknowledged that the forces at his disposal were by now too weak to attempt to get through and join those at the bridge, and the Oosterbeek Perimeter began to form. The Perimeter was roughly thumb-shaped with the base resting on the River Rhine, and Div. HQ in the centre. It stretched from the river northwards to the railway line, some 2,000 metres, and was about 1,600 metres across at the widest point. What was left of the three Brigades were now deployed in the defence of this Perimeter as the enemy closed in around them.

Prisoners were still being brought into the Airlanding Brigade HQ to be quickly disarmed and searched before the Provost NCOs escorted them to Div. HQ for interrogation. Corporal Jock Moir tells of one group he escorted there:

> *We weren't too far from Div. HQ so it didn't take too long to get there, dodging the shelling all the time. We were all pretty tired and we were supposed to start digging trenches when we got there. I thought that it would be a good job for the prisoners to do, so I handed some shovels out to them and tried to explain what I wanted them to do. They must have thought that I wanted them to dig their own graves, because they flatly refused and started to get a bit stroppy. Anyway, I took one of them round the corner, handed him over to some Paras in a trench, then fired a couple of shots in to the air. I went back to the prisoners on my own and they must have thought that I'd shot their mate because they started digging like mad.*

The buildings housing Brigade HQ were now under almost constant attack from mortars and shellfire. A direct hit on the HQ during a conference on Wednesday morning killed a number of Staff Officers including the Defence Platoon Commander. But the danger didn't only come from the enemy shellfire. During a re-supply drop in to the Brigade area on the Thursday afternoon the aircraft was badly shot-up by flak and ME109s. A container of 6 Pounder ammunition dropped free and landed on Brigade HQ and the ensuing explosion wounded a number of Military Policemen who were in the vicinity. Dennis Fitzgerald was dug well in at the time and escaped injury, but he saw what happened to one of the other NCOs:

I remember big Lcpl Charles getting hit. When the container blew up he got a lump of shrapnel in his thigh and stood there in the open taking his trousers off to put a dressing on the wound. We were not under fire at the time but, with Gerry less than 100 yards away, there he stood in the open with his trousers round his ankles. Before he could finish what he was doing the firing started up again and he just stood there, trying to pull his trousers up and waving his fist in the direction of the Gerries calling them all the names under the sun.

The Polish Brigade were due to land on the 19th with the 3rd Lift but had also fallen victim to the English weather and could not take off until the 21st. Their planned DZ was south of the river and close to the bridge but, as this area was still in enemy hands, the Brigade dropped beside the village of Driel directly across the river from the Perimeter at Oosterbeek. As expected, they received a hot reception from the enemy on the south side of the river and the DZ was swept by machine gun and mortar fire. In addition, a number of Dakotas had been shot down during the flight in and around 40 had been forced to return to England through bad weather, taking with them a full battalion of Polish Paratroopers. Only around 200 of the brave Poles managed to cross the river to assist the beleaguered British in the Perimeter, mainly in the area of the Schoonoord cross-roads.

On Friday the 22nd heavy shelling of Brigade HQ resulted in the wounding of two further Staff Officers and it was decided to vacate the badly damaged houses and to move the HQ deeper in to the wooded area behind the Hartenstein. One report stated:

The final location of Brigade HQ was in a little wood close to a small lake. It was always under fire and we lived very much underground. In those circumstances it is advisable to arrange for everything to be underground. Our cookhouse wasn't, to our great regret.
Food was something of a problem, towards the end of the week, and there were some ducks on the lake. It is surprising how difficult it is to kill a duck, even with a Sten, and even

when they are dead they remain afloat with their legs up out in the middle and you aren't much better off. But the wind gradually carried some of he bodies ashore. We found a hip-bath and some potatoes and apples and if it was not to be roast duck and apple sauce it was to be a stew with the same ingredients. It was a nice stew and just when it was ready a mortar bomb burst on the cookhouse roof and precipitated the roof into the stew. Fortunately no one was hurt on that occasion.

The abridged War Diary of the Headquarters 1st Airlanding Brigade records the 23rd and 24th Saturday and Sunday as follows:

Days of continuous mortaring and shelling which resulted in a steady drain of men. Reports from units showed a rapid decrease in numbers caused by this and continuous attacks by infantry, tanks, including flame throwers and SP guns. All attacks were repulsed with the assistance of the medium guns from 30 Corps. Nevertheless snipers and SP guns succeeded in infiltrating behind most units and even established themselves in a position 100 yards from the Brigade HQ, from which they could not be dislodged. Lieutenant Austin and a number of valuable NCOs of Brigade HQ were killed on the 24th trying to drive them back.

On Monday the 25th Dennis Fitzgerald and Peter Downton escorted the Brigadier on a dash to Div. HQ where the General issued the instructions that the Division was to pull out and cross to the south of the river that night. When they returned to Brigade HQ they found one of the MPs guarding a newly captured German prisoner. Dennis Fitzgerald explains:

He was a big fellow wearing a black uniform. He was off one of the Self-Propelled guns that had been giving us so much trouble and I seem to recall that he had given himself up because he was smiling and saying things like ... "No more war. I have children" .. then he pulled out these pictures of his wife and kids and started showing them around. I thought,

No 3 Section (1st Airlanding Brigade)

hell, they're giving themselves up, and we're about to pull out.

When Jock Moir received the news that they were pulling out he was with the remains of the KOSB Battalion at the northern edge of the rapidly shrinking Perimeter. Earlier he had been called upon to give covering fire from his Bren when the hard-pressed KOSB had charged the enemy at the point of the bayonet to clear their position. Not many survived that charge, and Jock Moir cannot understand to this day how he came out of it alive. And then the last of his ammunition had gone:

I had to get rid of the Bren. I couldn't carry it with me if we were pulling out and I had no ammo left anyway. I slung the bolt away as far as I could, then buried the Bren. We also buried one of the KOSB lads there, a Sergeant out of the HQ Section. We buried him beside a little stream that ran through the wood. There was a small building, a little house I think, and we buried him close by that, about 5 yards from the water. I've often wondered if they found his grave when the war was over. During that last afternoon I captured a Gerry as we were walking through the wood. I remember that he was a veteran of North Africa and could speak a little English. Because we thought that he might have guessed we were getting ready to pull out we decided to keep him with us and take him back over the water that night.

On that last day in the Perimeter Lcpl Dennis Riley was seriously wounded in the head by shrapnel. He had narrowly escaped injury on several occasions at Brigade HQ when he preferred to remain in his slit trench outside rather than shelter inside the building. Now he was rushed to the Medical Dressing Station where he was reunited with his mates injured by the exploding 6 Pounder ammunition a few days earlier. They were all to be taken into captivity when the remains of the Division evacuated that night.

At 1pm on Monday the 25th the Brigade Commander issued orders to his Staff for Operation Berlin, the evacuation of the Division. The Brigade HQ Group were to rendezvous at the small lake in the woods at 11pm that evening and to make their way down to the river. After 8 days of intense and brutal fighting, of being assaulted by infantry, tanks, artillery, flame throwers and aircraft, the exhausted, hungry but still determined paratroopers were being pulled out. The Perimeter had been gradually reduced in size by the unrelenting pressure of the enemy. A breakthrough by German armour at the base of the Perimeter had threatened to cut off the Division's last escape route over the river, but artillery fire and aircraft attacks had halted the armour.

Many of the Division's wounded lay in the crowded cellars of the Hartenstein. Others outside in slit trenches, in shattered private houses and in the Medical Stations within the perimeter. Amongst them were a number of the Provost Officers and NCOs. To a man the Doctors and Chaplains of the Division elected to remain behind with the wounded and take their chances. They would not be joining the evacuation that night.

Arrangements had been made for the artillery of 30 Corps south of the river to lay down a barrage of fire to cover the withdrawal. Routes down to the river's edge through the shattered trees and rubble-strewn paths were marked with tape and, as darkness fell, the men began to slip quietly from their trenches and head towards freedom. Holding the hand or the coat-tail of the man in front, boots wrapped in whatever cloth was available to muffle the sound, they stumbled wearily through the darkness. As if to aid the evacuation that night was dark with a strong wind and driving rain which helped to hide any possible noise from the withdrawing paratroopers. Some of the wounded who were still able to hold a weapon remained in the trenches around the Perimeter, firing as long as the ammunition held out, and making occasional radio transmissions to give the enemy the impression that all was normal.

Of the one Officer and 12 NCOs of the Provost Section who had landed with the Brigade on the 17th, only Lt. Horton and five of the NCOs returned across the river that night. Dennis Fitzgerald was one of them:

> *When it came time for us to pull out Peter Downton and I were with the Brigadier and his Batman. We eventually reached the river bank and there was already quite a crowd*

gathered there. We took the Brigadier right down to the water's edge and he sent the three of us off to get in to one of the boats. The boats were being operated by British and Canadian Engineers and I can't tell you how glad we were to see them. We got about half-way across and the boat started drifting in the fast current down river. We had gone quite a way down before we could get in to the south bank. We made our way back along the bank towards the spot where we should have landed, then to Driel where somebody gave me a blanket and half a tin of cold stew. It tasted brilliant. Some time later we met up with our lads from the Seaborne Element down at Nijmegan. I also saw our Brigadier there and it was the only time I heard him swear. He was limping and said ... "Some bloody fool trod on my foot".

Jock Moir was another of the fortunate ones who got away to the safety of the south bank that night:

I don't remember very much of how we got down to the river that night. I know that I had the German prisoner with me and I was determined that he was coming along as well. I do remember how cold and wet it was, and then, when we were in the small boats crossing the river, putting my hand in the water and thinking how warm it felt. Once on the other bank we stumbled out of the boat and made our way to Driel. It didn't seem long before I bumped in to a couple of our lads from the Seaborne Element, so they must have been quite close up to the river that night.

The evacuation ceased at first light as the Germans realised that the Division had slipped out of the net. The river bank was raked by machine gun fire and many of the small boats, manned by the tireless Sappers, were blown from the water. Over three-quarters of the Airlanding Brigade HQ remained on the north bank some attempting to battle against the strong current and swim across. Very few made it. Of the 3 battalions plus Support Troops who had arrived with the 1st Lift, the Brigade could muster less than the equivalent of a battalion when it reached Nijmegen.

```
                                    THE WAR OFFICE (CAS. P.W.)
                                    Curzon Street House,
                                    Curzon Street,
                                    London, W.1.

SS/11/591 (Cas.P.W.)                26th October, 1944.

Madam,

        I am directed to inform you that the following item was included
in a broadcast from German European Service on  25th October, 1944,:

        "Names of members of 1st Airborne Division (Wounded):
        L/Cpl. Dennis Riley, sends his love to his Mother, 8, Darnley
        St., Old Trafford, Manchester."


        Will you please be good enough to verify or furnish the service
particulars (e.g. Rank, Army number and Unit) of the soldier to whom
the broadcast refers, if these are known to you, quoting the above
reference in your reply. An envelope label which does not require a
stamp is enclosed for your use.

        It is pointed out that the broadcasts from foreign sources are not
the recognised official channels for communicating information, and that
on occasion they have been found to be unreliable.

        When corresponding with Lance/Corporal Riley,    please do not
mention that this was a broadcast report.


                            I am,
Mrs. Riley or Occupier,     Sir/Madam,
   8, Darnley Street,          Your obedient Servant,
      Old Trafford,
        Manchester.
```

The letter informing Mrs Riley of her son's capture.

CHAPTER 7

COMPANY HQ AND NUMBER 4 SECTION (ATT. TO DIV. HQ)

Look at these British troops, you don't see any of them grumbling

(German Officer in the Div. HQ POW Cage)

For Operation Market-Garden Div. HQ had the largest allocation of Provost resources. Major O.P. Haig held the appointment of Assistant Provost Marshal on the HQ Staff with Lcpl 'Flash' Pulford and his Batman/Driver. Also attached were Lcpls Jackie Mole and 'Paddy' Breen as motor cycle escorts to the Divisional Commander, Major General R.E. Urquhart DSO. The escort were to travel by glider with the General on the 1st Lift, Sunday the 17th.

The reduced Company HQ Section comprised the Officer Commanding, Captain W.B. 'Jock' Gray, RSM Bill Kibble, Sgt. Ernie Howard, (the orderly room Sgt.), and Lcpls Langton and Nunn as Batmen/Drivers. Corporal Ivor Stride was the Section cook.

For Security Duties, Escorts, Prisoner of War Cage and any additional duties, Number 4 Section was brought up to full strength for the Operation. The Section was commanded by Lieutenant R.J. Falck of the Parachute Regiment who was also the unit Intelligence Officer. He was a German speaking Dutchman who would act as Liaison Officer with the civilian population and as the interrogator of any POWs. The Section was made up of Sgt. Yardley, Corporals

Peter Dale and 'Ginger' Hodgson, with Lcpls Cressy, Evans, Hackett, Haycock, Hookway, Hope, Jones, Newby, Pentney, Reast, Storry, Thelwall and Unsworth.

The Provost element flew in to Arnhem over two days with the 1st and 2nd Lifts, some arriving by parachute from Barkston Heath and Saltby, others by glider from airfields in the South of England. On landing the Company HQ Section were co-located with Div. HQ and established a Provost Company Headquarters. Number 4 Section were to assist with the marshalling and dispersal of vehicles and men on the DZs and LZs, then to join up with Div. HQ for further duties. As has already been described in previous chapters, those arriving on the 17th had an uneventful flight in, and a relatively peaceful reception on landing with a minimum of unfriendly fire. The heat was to be turned up before the arrival of the 2nd Lift.

Lcpl Tom 'Paddy' Breen was a 26 year old ex-Royal Engineer who had already seen service in Iceland, North Africa and Italy. Now he found himself with his mate Jackie Mole in a glider being towed from Fairford to a patch of earth west of Arnhem. As motor cycle escorts to the General they travelled with him in one of the first gliders to land. Also in the glider was the General's ADC, his Batman Frank Hancock, a signaller, the General's Jeep and the two Police motor cycles. It was very soon after landing and clearing the glider that the two Military Policemen discovered that their Matchless 350cc bikes were having difficulty keeping up with the General's Jeep as it raced around the narrow lanes and sandy tracks. General Urquhart quickly dispensed with his outriders and the two NCO's were absorbed in to Number 4 Section for general Police Duties at Div. HQ.

As the daylight faded on that first day Div. HQ and the Military Policemen who had arrived with the 1st Lift settled down for the night in the now empty gliders on the LZ. The General, minus his MP escort, had already left with his signaller in the Jeep to check on the progress of the 1st Brigade as they fought their way towards Arnhem and the bridge. At dawn the following day Div. HQ moved off the LZ and took up a position some 2km away beside the Utrechtseweg leading to Oosterbeek. The General had not yet returned and the HQ were having no success in their attempts to

Company HQ and No 4 Section (Att to Div. HQ)

contact him by radio. (They were not to know that the previous night his Jeep had received a direct hit from a mortar bomb and that his signaller had been seriously wounded). General Urquhart was not to rejoin his Headquarters until 7.30am on the 19th having been 'missing' for over 36 hours, most of the time spent surrounded by the enemy and trapped in a house close to St Elizabeth's Hospital. Brigadier Lathbury, who had been wounded, was trapped in a similar house 75 yards to the west.

Meanwhile, the delayed 2nd Lift brought in the majority of the Div. HQ Provost NCOs. Amongst them was Cpl Harold Bennet on Number 1 Section with the Section Jeep and Trailer. His orders were to head straight for the main Police Station at Arnhem. He explains what happened next:

> *The glider I was in crash landed rather heavily and shook us up quite a bit. Although no-one was killed or badly injured we had to smash our way out of the wreckage then recover the Jeep, trailer and stores. My instructions were to make for the Police Station and link up with Sgt Callaway but I soon found that this was no longer possible as all the routes in to town were cut off by the enemy. I tried a couple of alternative routes but found that it was impossible to get through, so I then joined up with Div. HQ at the Hartenstein and dug in there hoping that I could join up with my own Section later.*

Lcpl Harry Wilce travelled in the same glider as RSM Bill Kibble and a number of other Provost NCOs, plus the Section Jeep. The first couple of hours in the air were quite a pleasant experience before they reached the coast of Holland, but very nearly ended in disaster for one of the passengers. Harry Wilce explains:

> *There were a couple of long sheets of steel in the floor of the glider to use as ramps when we were unloading the Jeep, the glider side door was wide open and the RSM sat facing it. He got up to have a look through the door as we crossed the coast and his studded boots started sliding on the steel plates. I grabbed hold of his webbing and, with a bit of assistance*

from two of the lads we managed to pull him away from the door.

We cast off from the tug over the LZ and the pilot made quite a good landing. We had all been well drilled in the correct method of detaching the tail of the glider, sliding the metal channels into position and driving the Jeep out, only this time things didn't quite go right. We couldn't shift the bolts on the tail at all so the Jeeps had to be manhandled by brute force and ignorance out of the entrance door at the side. Corporal Hodgson, our Section Corporal, rode one of the motor cycles out of the glider and raced off shouting that he was going to get himself a medal. There was a lot of enemy action around the area and within a couple of minutes he received a lump of shrapnel in his behind.

Stanley Reast who had spent part of the summer helping the Lincolnshire farmers with their harvesting, parachuted in with the 2nd Lift. He remembers the warm welcome which awaited them:

As we were approaching the DZ I looked through the small window in the plane and saw the bullets coming up through the wing, just like stitching. We got the order to 'Hook up' and we all shuffled forward towards the open door. As we moved forward towards the exit the chap in front of me was hit just as he reached the door. I pushed him out of the way and leapt into space, glad to be clear of the aircraft. I remember Major Haig being with us in the aircraft and passing round a bottle of whisky.

On that Monday afternoon the DZs and LZs were raked by gunfire as the Germans attacked from all sides. Aircraft were shot out of the sky before they could deliver their passengers, and plunged to earth in a ball of flame. Paratroopers leapt from aircraft, glad to be free of the noise and claustrophobic confinement, only to meet a hail of bullets fired up at them from the trees surrounding the DZ as the enemy sprayed the sky with Spandau and rifle fire. The CMP suffered their first fatality of the battle on that day when Lcpl Hookway was shot as he descended by parachute. He died still

Company HQ and No 4 Section (Att to Div. HQ)

in his parachute harness, suspended in the trees beside the DZ. Harry Wilce picks up the account of that day:

We were supposed to make our way to Div. HQ but it was all such a shambles. Nobody appeared to know where anyone else was. We got everything out of the glider and set off for the map reference we had been given. Somehow, I got separated from the rest of the lads and found myself following a tree-lined road which was running in the right direction. I met up with the tail end of a Parachute Battalion who were in the ditches at the side of the road, pinned down by heavy mortar fire. Eventually we moved on and came across a wrecked car holding a group of dead Germans who had been wiped out by 3 Para. I cut the shoulder epaulets off the Officer hanging out of the passenger door and handed them in for identification to a group of our Officers installed in a nearby building. I finally met up again with my own crowd, but still couldn't locate Div. HQ so we spent the night in a school. We were contacted there by a Dutchman who said he was with the Resistance and the following morning he guided us to Div. HQ which by now was at the Hartenstein Hotel.

By Wednesday morning all the CMP had reported in to Div. HQ and dug their trenches within the extensive grounds of the imposing Hotel. Provost Company HQ was established in a large trench suitably protected overhead with timber 'found' in the Hotel grounds. About 200 yards behind the Hotel, almost hidden amongst the trees, stood some tennis courts surrounded by a high wire-mesh fence. These were earmarked to hold enemy prisoners and trenches were dug on two sides of the courts for the CMP NCOs who were detailed to guard them. The APM, Major Haig, and his batman Lcpl 'Flash' Pulford were also dug in close to the tennis courts. The Policemen were also detailed to carry out security duties on the main entrance to the Hotel ensuring that the correct daily password 'Challenge' and 'Reply' was given. Stan Reast also remembers spending some time on Traffic Control trying to sort some order out of the chaos of vehicles parked around the Hotel. The situation involving the other Div. troops outside the Perimeter was so

Map 4
The Divisional Perimeter positions. Thursday 21st September 1944.

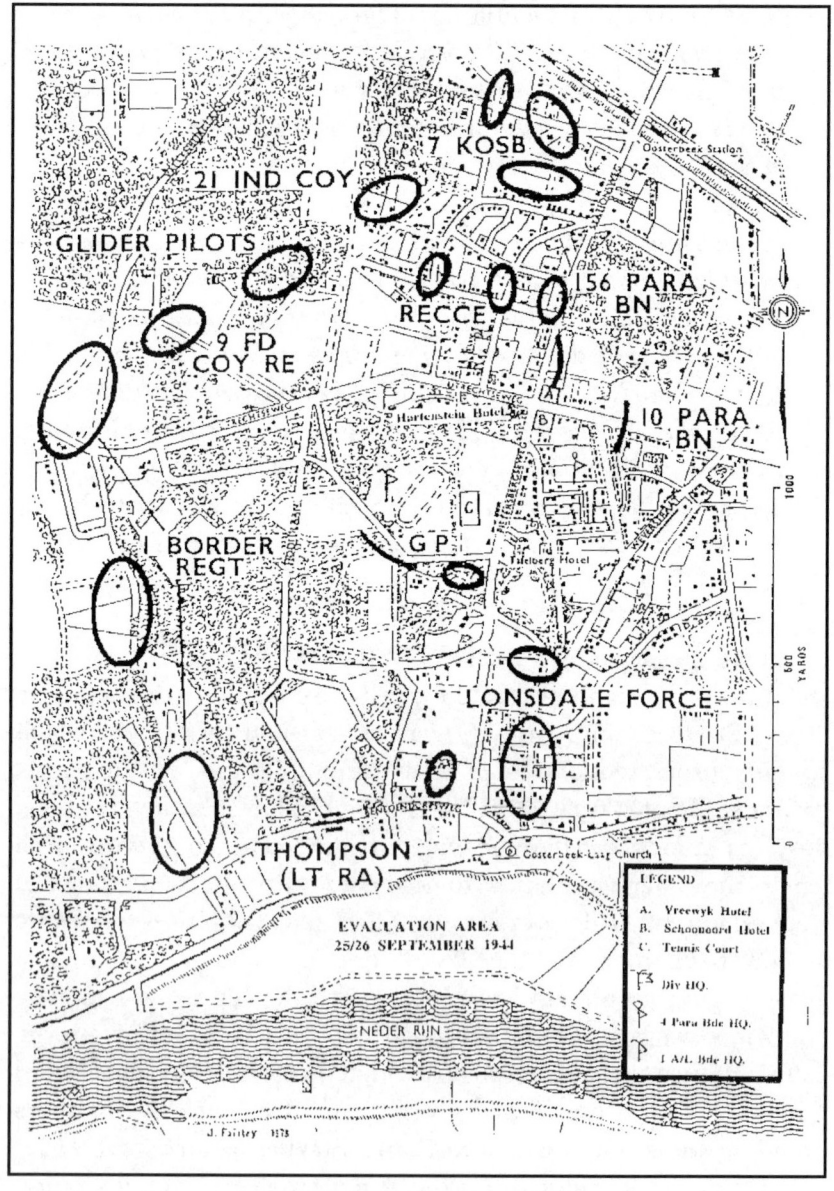

Company HQ and No 4 Section (Att to Div. HQ)

confused and fluid that, for most of the time, even the Staff Officers at Div. HQ did not know exactly what was happening. The troops in their slit trenches knew even less of the battle's progress.

Enemy prisoners were constantly being brought in to Div. HQ and by the 21st there were around 200 held in the tennis courts cage, including 4 females and 2 Officers. Of the remainder, 60% were from the SS and the rest from various Wehrmacht units with few between the ages of 20 and 40. Guarding the prisoners around the clock became the main duty of Number 4 Section. Stan Reast again:

> *I only remember one of the female prisoners as she was doing some cooking for the other prisoners on a bit of a Field Kitchen they had set up. There was also a high-ranking Officer there as a prisoner. He had his own little dug-out with a thick cover on top and he always disappeared in there when the shelling was about to start. I was there one day when the prisoners were grumbling and the Officer came over to tell them off. He said ... "Look at these British troops, you don't see any of them grumbling". Lt Falck was with me at the time and translated all that the German was saying. I shared some of my tobacco with the German Officer, he was all right.*

Sturmbannfeurer Sepp Kraft's SS Panzer Grenadier Training and Depot Battalion were responsible for the ambush of the Recce Squadron beside the railway at Wolfheze and for the initial delaying of the 1st Parachute Brigade advance. The Battalion had suffered considerable casualties in the first few days of the battle and had been reinforced by a mixture of Marines and Military Police. The unit's War Diary has this to say about the prisoners:

> *The enemy treated our prisoners quite well. They were caged in the tennis courts near to Oosterbeek and were there exposed to our own heavy firing. Food supply was short, but so it was for the British as well. They were nearly starving. Valuables like rings and watches were always taken away, but papers were given back after examination. The British*

> *expect soldierly bearing and discipline, even from prisoners. The British Divisional Commander is said to have appeared on the tennis courts one day and told the (German) prisoners that if they did not show more soldierly bearing and discipline he would have them all locked up.*
>
> *Searching of the prisoners was superficial. One of the German NCOs kept a grenade in his trouser pocket and escaped by killing his guard with it.*

The prisoners had also to be fed, as well as guarded, and there was barely sufficient food for the British. Most of the re-supply drops, it will be recalled, were falling in to German hands and the Paras were forced to forage for food wherever they could. Major Haig took 'Paddy' Breen and Jackie Mole to raid a nearby turnip field searching for food for the Company and the prisoners. They managed to unearth a few meagre turnips which took away the pangs of hunger for a couple of hours. Harry Wilce remembers the euphoria and anticipation he felt when a small re-supply canister dropped close enough to the POW cage to be recovered. Two of the NCOs dragged it towards their trench and forced open the catches which had jammed on landing. Their efforts were rewarded with a supply of plastic cap badges and copies of the previous Sunday's newspapers.

Life in the grounds of the Hartenstein Hotel was fast becoming one of survival and there was soon no question of Div. HQ following the Brigade troops in to Arnhem. On the morning of Wednesday the 20th the enemy bombardment of the Perimeter began in earnest and was to continue for the next six days and nights. It is estimated that at one point, no fewer than 117 guns from 4 German Artillery Regiments were firing in to the confined area held by the British. Buildings were systematically reduced to heaps of smouldering rubble, proud trees, torn asunder like so much matchwood, lay in tangled heaps. Carefully tended fields and gardens were instantly transformed in to mounds of earth and stones. Amid all this carnage and destruction the Military Policemen, together with cooks, drivers, clerks, signallers and anyone else who could hold and aim a rifle, fought to defend the territory around Div. HQ and to stay alive. Only a few short days before they had been enjoying

Company HQ and No 4 Section (Att to Div. HQ)

the hospitality of a Lincolnshire pub, now they crouched, tired and hungry, in holes dug deep in to the sandy Dutch soil. The sweet smell of the pine trees had given way to the heavy stench of cordite and burning wood as the enemy attacked relentlessly. Of all the weapons in the enemy's arsenal the most feared was the Nebelwerfer, a six barrelled mortar whose bombs made a distinctive screaming noise as they fell onto the trenches of the waiting British, often bursting in the trees overhead and showering those below with a rain of searing shrapnel.

Joe Robinson, one of a handful of survivors of R Company of the 1st Parachute Battalion, remembers an unnamed Military Policeman who was fighting elsewhere in the Perimeter:

He joined us at Oosterbeek Old Church with the Lonsdale Force and fought alongside us until the night we were evacuated, then he left to join the MPs guarding the prisoners. I never knew his name but those lads were amongst the last to leave the Perimeter. Some made it over the Rhine, and some didn't.

Corporal Harold Bennett, unable to join his Section at the Police Station, had linked up with Number 4 Section around the POW Cage. He recalls his last day in the Perimeter:

I was dodging across one of the lawns coming back from the Hotel when this mortar landed a couple of feet in front of me. In that split second I thought my time had come, but the thing went off and all I got was a shower of earth. Not a scratch on me. I thought that if I could survive that, then I could survive anything. I raced back to my trench which was next to one occupied by the BBC War Correspondents and listened to Stanley Maxted making one of his famous recordings.

Later that day whilst I was on Stand-To in the trench a shell burst close by and I was hit by lumps of shrapnel in my elbow, shoulder and thigh. I injected myself with the Morphine which we all carried, then someone took me to the Medics in the cellar of the Hotel. I was in a pretty bad way and the next thing I knew I was being treated by some Dutch ladies in a house. They cut off my bloody and filthy battle dress, dressed my wounds as best they could, and gave me some clean civilian clothing to wear. I was strapped to a stretcher, which was loaded onto the bonnet of a Jeep, then driven through the streets to St. Elizabeth Hospital where the wounded of both sides were being treated. I shall never forget the bravery of that Medic who drove me to the hospital. There was shelling and firing going on all around, buildings collapsing and everywhere seemed to be on fire, yet somehow he got us through. Like thousands of others I owe my life to that British Medic.

I remember lying on the ground at the hospital and some big German pointing a gun at my head. I thought he was going to shoot me because I was wearing civilian clothes. I managed to get my Red Beret out of my pocket and pull out the 'Dog Tags' from around my neck. He lowered the gun and walked away. And that was the end of my war. After the Division had evacuated on the 25th all of the wounded were moved to Apeldoorn and from there to POW camps in Germany.

By the end of the first week the situation inside the Perimeter was desperate. The defenders were without food and water, ammunition was in very short supply and medical equipment practically non-existent. The Medical Dressing Stations housed at the Vreewyk and Schoonoord Hotels, either side of Oosterbeek cross roads where Stationsweg joins Utrechtseweg and only 300 meters from Div. HQ, had both fallen in to enemy hands. First Aid Posts had also been established in the Tafelberg Hotel on Pietersbergseweg and in the home of Kate ter Horst and her family beside the Oosterbeek Old Church. The number of wounded had mounted steadily throughout the week and now conditions inside these buildings was appalling. Every available foot of space was packed with stretchers holding wounded. Those who couldn't find a stretcher lay on the floor or outside on the grass as they waited for their turn to be attended to. Operations were often performed by torchlight, and a sip of clean water became a luxury to be savoured. The dead lay wherever space could be found, moved outside to make way for the living. After the war the bodies of 57 paratroopers were moved from the hastily dug graves in the trim garden of Kate ter Horst's house.

For those still manning the trenches around the Perimeter an additional danger came from the many snipers who had infiltrated through their stretched lines of defence and camouflaged themselves in the trees and bushes. The Paras were picked off through telescopic sights as they moved around inside the Perimeter. They crawled cautiously from their trenches to search for the snipers, matching them at their own game as they scanned the trees for the tell-tale of a wisp of smoke or the glint of a weapon.

The toll of Military Police wounded increased as they dodged the shells and bullets to go about their duties. Both Major Haig and RSM Kibble were wounded by shrapnel as they toured the trenches encouraging the young Policemen, the RSM being the more seriously injured of the two. He managed to make his own way to a RAMC First Aid Post, but as he entered by the front door a group of SS Grenadiers entered by the back and he was taken prisoner. A mortar bomb fell close to the trench Harry Wilce was sharing with Stan Reast and Joe Unsworth depositing a lump of shrapnel in Harry's arm. He climbed out of the trench clutching his bleeding arm and shouting ... "They can't hit me again, I've already been wounded" ... Then he walked to the First Aid Post for treatment, but quickly returned to the trench when he saw just how many seriously wounded were there already.

On the afternoon of Monday the 25th, Lcpl Stan Reast was on Security Duty inside the Hartenstein Hotel when an Officer shouted to him to leave his post and man one of the windows:

> *As I walked over towards the window the remains of the glass in the frame was blown in by an explosion. I pushed a settee across the window for cover and settled down to watch the driveway. Then Corporal Dale came in and told me to report to our Company HQ trench right away. Captain Gray was there and he just said that the Division would be pulling out over the river that night, but that the Military Police would be staying behind to guard the prisoners after the Div. HQ left. He explained that, if we **all** left then the prisoners would*

raise the alarm if they realised that we had gone. After the rest started pulling out we stayed behind until about 11pm then two of the single lads, Peter Dale and Ken Storry said that they would stay behind on their own to give the rest of us a chance to get away. I think there was also a Dutch Officer who stayed with them, but it wasn't Lt. Falck.

About 10pm that night the evacuation began with boats of the Canadian and British Sappers carrying the wounded across first. Then followed a continuous shuttle of fragile, overloaded assault boats as the task began of rescuing over 2,000 red-eyed, gaunt and exhausted survivors. In the grounds of Div. HQ the remains of the ammunition was gathered together and blown up. Breech blocks and sights were removed from the guns and destroyed. The inky blackness, together with the wind and incessant rain, helped to cover the noise as the grim defenders made their way slowly down towards the river bank, guided by the lines of tape and the reassuring directions of the indefatigable Glider Pilots. Small groups of men felt their way cautiously forward over fallen trees and along paths made slippery by the rain. All that was left of Companies and Battalions, Border Regiment, KOSB, 10th and 156th Battalions from the 4th Brigade, Sappers, Recce Squadron, men of the 21st Independent Company who had been the first to land and mark the DZs, Gunners who had fought so valiantly and who had then to destroy their own guns. All followed the paths down to the river and the hoped for safety of the south bank.

Stan Reast joined the small group of Military Policemen beside the Company HQ trench. Captain Gray did a quick head count, saddened at how few of the Section remained, then checked that the men's boots had been muffled and all loose equipment had been secured. The small party set off towards the river. Stan Reast tells what happened next:

There was perhaps a dozen of us, maybe more. There was tape for us to follow and I was up near the front with Captain Gray. We came to a small cross-roads and were half way over when they opened up on us. The bullets ploughed in to our group and Sergeant Yardley yelled for us to scatter and regroup on the far side of the road. It was all noise and confusion and I ran hell for leather and jumped off the road for cover. I landed in some barbed wire strands which were stretched across the track between the trees. I had my small pack on and was carrying my Sten and somehow I managed to get tangled up in the barbed wire. While I was struggling to get free the Germans opened up on us again and there were bullets flying everywhere. It was pitch dark, but suddenly it appeared to be as bright as day. I think they'd probably put a flare up. I thought the only thing to do was to play dead so I dropped my arms and just hung there. I could hear the bullets whistling over my head and smacking into the trees, but I was lucky and they all missed me.

When it quietened down a bit I managed to struggle free. I could see the guns firing down by the river so I knew which direction I had to head in. I couldn't see anyone else from the Section so I set off on my own. I headed for the river, crawling along and dropping in to the occasional shell hole. Then it suddenly lit up all around me again and there was a bloody great German standing right in front of me and holding a stick grenade. But he never saw me. I was looking right at him thinking ... "This is it", ... But he carried on walking away from me. I backed away and rolled into a ditch full of water. I was wet through and remember thinking to myself ... "You silly bugger, you could get pneumonia"....After that there are a couple of hours missing in my memory. I know that I'd got some cracked ribs from somewhere, but I don't know where those couple of hours went to. The next thing I remember was that it was nearly daylight. The area was crawling with Gerries and it wasn't long before I was captured.

For many years John Hamblett and other ex-Airborne Military Policemen have been trying to find out what happened to the Dutch Intelligence Officer, Lt. Falck. His next-of-kin were anxious for information and John was eager to help. There is no grave in Oosterbeek Cemetery bearing his name and the POW records did not provide any information. Nobody who John contacted was able to provide positive proof of the Officer's fate on the night of the evacuation, although one story said that he had last been seen being led in to captivity with his eyes swathed in bandages. This proved to be untrue. Stan Reast had the answer when we managed to trace him in 1993.

> *After I was captured I was taken to a house which had been made in to a sort of First Aid Post. They put me in to a room with another of our CMP lads. Captain Gray was also there, very badly wounded. He had been shot the previous evening when we were caught at the crossroads. I went to put a Field Dressing on his wound and saw that the blood was all pink and frothy, so I knew that he hadn't got much of a chance. Anyway, I put another dressing on him and gave him some morphine, marking the details of the morphine on his forehead. I sat with him for a while before I was taken off to a small hospital. It was in a converted schoolroom or something like that, and the Doctor there looked me over but all I had was some blood on my face from the struggle with the barbed wire, nothing serious. He then sent me with some other prisoners to fetch in a wounded RAF chap from the attic of a house down the road.*
>
> *A guard then took us back to the original house. Near this house I had seen Lt. Falck propped against a lamp post, dead. Lying close to him was Lcpl Newby, also dead. I asked the Germans if I could bury my Officer and comrade and they gave me two shovels and detailed the other MP to come with me.*
>
> *They sent us out under guard and we went across the road to where there was a big orchard by the side of a house. We buried the two of them there. This was somewhere on the route between the Hartenstein and the river. I know for certain that it was Lt. Falck because he had been with the Company for a few months and I had got to know him. Also, when I searched his body I found that he didn't have any identification 'Dog Tags' on. Perhaps this was because he was a Dutchman, or he had simply taken them off. Anyway, all I could find as proof of his identity was his cheque book. I*

eventually handed this to a British Officer who questioned us in the Prison Camp. I also took one of Jack Newby's 'Dog Tags' as proof of ID.

At no time when I was first captured was I interrogated. I think the Germans who captured us initially were forward troops and they were probably unsure what to do with us. A group of us were made to go down through the woods at the rear of the Hartenstein and clear away the barbed wire our boys had laid, and to pick up any mines we found. I'd never had anything to do with mines before so I wasn't too keen on the idea.

Some time later we were marched with other prisoners to the Railway Station and loaded in to cattle trucks. We spent several days in the trucks on the way in to Germany. They let us out of the trucks once a day to stretch our legs, but left us locked inside every time there was an RAF raid.

Lcpl 'Paddy' Breen, one of the General's motor cycle escort, was also with the group of Policemen ambushed at the cross roads:

I was in the line heading for the river and walking just behind Lcpl Jones when we were attacked at the cross roads. We dashed across the road when the firing started and dived into a ditch or a dug-out together. After a while, after the firing had stopped, we climbed out and headed off down the road. We hadn't gone very far when a grenade or shell exploded right next to us. I took the blast full in the face and Jones was wounded quite badly. He was screaming at the Germans, but he died pretty soon afterwards lying there next to me in the road. I lay there all night in the gutter unable to see a thing. Some time later I heard heavy footsteps and then a big German boot pushed me over onto my back. Someone put a bottle in my hands and I took a swig. My teeth were chattering together with the cold and the whisky, or whatever it was, warmed me up a bit. I was taken on a stretcher to a hospital at Apeldoorn north of Arnhem where I had some attention to my eyes and ears. From there it was over the border into Germany and a German Military Hospital, then on to a hospital in Frankfurt and finally to one at Obermassfeld where the 1st Airborne Medics were attending to a lot of our wounded. In November that year they said that I was fit enough to go in to the POW Camp at Muhlhausen.

>
> Reference:-
> CMP/Div.III/13.
>
> R.A.(CA & SL) &
> C.M.P. Records,
> Savoy Hotel,
> West Hill Road,
> Bournemouth.
>
> 26th Feb.1945.
>
> Mrs. M. Breen,
> Whitby,
> 23, Hilldale Road,
> Cheam, SURREY.
>
> Dear Madam,
>   1917769 L/Cpl. BREEN T.
>
>   Further to my notification of the 25th February 1945, I have to inform you that the War Office has received information through the British Red Cross Society to the effect that your husband was admitted to Stalag IXB on the 26th October 1944.
>
>   The British Medical Officer in this Camp reports that L/Cpl. Breen was suffering from injuries due to blast. His eyes are affected but there will be practically no visual defect when his treatment is completed.
>
>   He has incurred an injury to the tympanic membrane of his left ear which is likely to be permanent, though causing only very slight deafness of the affected ear. His general health and spirits are reported to be excellent.
>
>   I trust you are receiving reassuring news direct from your husband.
>
>   Please notify this office of any change of Camp address which you may receive.
>
>   Yours faithfully,
> AK/EEG   i/c for Colonel
>   C.M.P.Records.

Information on the wounded was sometimes slow in coming through.

Company HQ and No 4 Section (Att to Div. HQ)

Cpl Peter Dale and Lcpl Ken Storry, who had remained behind guarding the prisoners in the tennis courts, crept away just before 1.30am that morning. The cold wind and slanting rain, together with the deafening box-barrage being put down around the Perimeter by the guns of 30 Corps to aid the evacuation, combined to ensure that the German prisoners kept their heads down. The two NCOs made their way down to the river alone and in almost darkness then, throwing off their heavy mud-stained clothing, they swam to the safety of the south bank.

Both men were recommended for awards for their unselfish actions that night, but our research has only been able to confirm that Peter Dale was awarded the Dutch Bronze Cross and was Mentioned in Dispatches. The citation reads:

> *After landing by parachute in the Arnhem area on the 18th September 1944, Corporal Dale, notwithstanding the fact that the Dropping Zone was swept by enemy fire, showed complete disregard for his personal safety by searching the area and rendering first aid to the wounded. Subsequently, on the night of 25/26 September, Corporal Dale volunteered to remain behind to guard some 200 Prisoners of War, and thus prevent any possibility of their escape interfering with the withdrawal of the Division. He remained under increasingly heavy fire. Only when the last parties were well clear, Corporal Dale made his way down to the river through enemy lines and swam to the south bank, as no boats were available. During the whole of the very exacting operation his coolness and cheerful disposition were an inspiration to those around him.*

The evacuation ceased at dawn on the 26th when the assault boats became too easy a target for the German guns. Under the cloak of darkness nearly 2,400 men had been taken across to safety. There still remained over 300 on the north bank, many to be captured as the enemy closed in, others to escape into the shelter of the woods to try again another night. Of the 3 Officers, I Warrant Officer and 24 Other Ranks of the Provost Company who fought with Div. HQ within the Perimeter, 2 Officers and 3 Other Ranks were killed, 1 Officer and 6 Other Ranks were evacuated, and the Warrant Officer plus 15 Other Ranks were taken in to captivity.

On the afternoon of 27th September, the survivors were addressed at Nijmegen by the Commander of the British 1st Airborne Corps, Lieutenant General F.A.M. 'Boy' Browning. They had been well fed, well rested and issued with new uniforms delivered by the Seaborne Element. By Saturday the 30th September they had all been flown back to the UK.

CHAPTER 8

THE EVADERS AND OPERATION PEGASUS

"Like a herd of stampeding elephants"
(Major Tatham-Warter)

When the evacuation of the Perimeter ceased at dawn on the 26th there were still over 300 members of the Division remaining on the north bank of the river. In addition, over 2,000 wounded had been left behind with virtually the whole of the Division's Medical staff. These included about 25 Officers and 400 Royal Army Medical Corps personnel and Battalion stretcher bearers. It is estimated that around 200 Airborne Officers and men went in to hiding that morning, some walking deep in to the woods, others hiding in the cellars of shattered buildings hoping to remain in hiding there until 30 Corps arrived. Many of the men had already been wounded earlier in the battle and had simply walked out of the German controlled hospitals during the confusion. One such was Brigadier G.W. Lathbury, the Commander of the 1st Parachute Brigade who had 'discharged' himself from the St. Elizabeth Hospital on the 26th.

On the night of the 22nd October 1944, just 4 weeks after the evacuation from the Perimeter, a further 15 Officers and 124 men, including a number of RAF Pilots, Americans, a Dutch Seaman, a Belgian and 3 Russians, escaped to the safety of the south bank of the Lower Rhine in Operation Pegasus. With them was Lcpl Wally Whitmill, a member of the ill-fated Number 1 Section which had been overrun at the main Arnhem Police Station on Tuesday the 19th September.

When the SS troops stormed the Police Station courtyard that afternoon there was total confusion amongst both attackers and defenders for a frantic few minutes. The enemy prisoners had been released from the cells and surged out in to the yard to greet their rescuers and to add to the turmoil. Wally Whitmill was guarding the window in one of the upper rooms at the time and in the chaos of shooting, yelling and exploding grenades he reasoned that there wasn't an awful lot he could do on his own against such odds. He took the opportunity to find a secure hiding place inside the building in the hope that he could eventually get back to friendly forces and live to fight another day. He was not to know that two others, Bob Peatling and Harry Parker from the Parachute Regiment, had similar thoughts and had also gone in to hiding for the time being. After a cursory search of the rooms the Germans marched their Military Police prisoners off in triumph. Lcpl Whitmill remained in hiding until darkness fell, then made good his escape in to the maze of narrow streets around the Police Station.

The people of Arnhem had suffered German occupation for the past 4 years and had naturally been overjoyed at the arrival of the British invaders. They were not to know just how badly the operation was going, or that within a few short days their would-be liberators would be lying dead, back south of the river, or in captivity. The gallant Dutch were only too aware that the penalty for assisting the British was death, and usually the whole family, but this did not deter them from doing all that they could to help those in hiding or on the run. Although they were desperately short themselves they were willing to share what little they had and provide shelter, clothing and food. Amongst the civilian population there were also a number of Nazi sympathisers who, once the fate of the British and the flow of battle became known, would have happily handed any paratrooper over to the Germans.

Wally Whitmill's exact movements during the next few hours must now be a matter of conjecture. A certain amount of information concerning his movements was given when he was de-briefed on the 23rd October following Operation Pegasus, but those few hours remain a mystery. What **is** known is that he was somehow led to the home of a Mr. Hueman, a baker on Joman Straat in Arnhem. Possibly one of the civilian Policemen, knowing that the Police Station had been overrun and the British marched away, returned that evening and, finding Whitmill in hiding, guided him to safety. Alternatively, as he was making good his escape under cover of darkness, he may have been lucky enough to fall in to the hands of the Dutch Resistance who took him to the nearest safe house. Whatever was the case, Wally was fortunate and the baker was sympathetic to the escaping soldier and provided food and shelter for a couple of days. He also fitted him out with a suit of rough civilian clothes.

The centre of the town was crawling with Germans and was not the place for an escaped British paratrooper to be. It was imperative that Wally, and any other soldiers found in hiding were moved in to the suburbs as soon as possible. Mr. Hueman made contact with a trusted Policeman who led Wally to the Arnhem suburb of Velp where he was handed over in to the care of a Mr. Radstaake, a nurseryman with premises on Ijsel Straat. There he remained for the next two weeks doing his best to keep out of sight during the day, and enjoying the hospitality and company of his hosts in the evening. Enemy patrols were constantly on the lookout for escaped paratroopers and downed aircrew and the nurseryman provided Wally with a bolt-hole should there be a surprise visit from one of the German patrols. The hiding place was in a recess half-way up one of the chimneys in a greenhouse and Wally frequently had to put this to good use during his stay with the Radstaakes. There was a particular close shave when a group of German soldiers entered the greenhouse when Wally was wedged in the chimney and were about to light a fire for warmth. Mr Radstaake somehow managed to talk them out of the idea.

Major A.J.Deane-Drummond MC was the Second in Command of the Divisional Signals and was captured on the 22nd September. He was taken to Velp along with a group of other British prisoners of war and placed in a large house prior to being transported across the border in to Germany. He managed to secrete himself inside a large cupboard when the rest of the prisoners were taken off to Germany, and locked the cupboard from the inside. He had with him only a small piece of bread and a bottle of water but, despite the fact that he could neither lie down now turn around in the cupboard, he remained there in hiding for 12 days. He eventually escaped from his self-imposed 'prison' and made contact with the Dutch Resistance who passed him from house to house for a few days until he was taken to a tiny semi-detached house in one of the side streets of Velp.

This was the home of Mr and Mrs Huisman and their two sons. Mr Huisman was a local primary school teacher in peacetime but was now devoting all his efforts to the Resistance and giving shelter to people, of various nationalities, who were on the run from the Germans. When Major Deane-Drummond arrived there were already two refugees hiding in the house, a Dutchman who had escaped from a Concentration Camp and a Polish/German Jew. With the arrival of the Major that made seven people in the cramped two-bedroomed house. When Wally Whitmill was also smuggled in to the house around the middle of October the Huismans welcomed him with open arms. Of course they would make room for him. He would be fed and he would be cared for.

A special hiding place had been constructed under the floorboards in the front room by cutting away a section of the boards. Bedding was a layer of quilts laid on the bare earth and access was by lifting the cut-away boards which could be quickly replaced once the men were safely down the hole, and covered by the carpet and settee. There was little chance of the hiding place being discovered by anything but the most thorough of searches, and the neighbours always gave early warning of any enemy patrols in the area.

The electricity and gas supplies to the house had long since been cut off so all cooking had to be done on a wood stove, but somehow Mrs Huisman managed to provide everyone with at least one hot meal a day. The 'lodgers' who could not leave the shelter of the house, helped by chopping firewood, preparing what vegetables there were, and generally helping around the house to keep themselves occupied.

Meanwhile plans were being made to gather all the British evaders together to mount a second evacuation across the river. One hundred members of the Division, including a number of Senior Officers, were in hiding at Ede, about 18km west of Arnhem, a further 50 were hidden in the outskirts of the town, and around 100 in the Arnhem area. Contact had been made with 30 Corps HQ south of the river, and a date set for what was to be known as Operation Pegasus. The evaders were to be assembled at various collecting points and guided to the crossing point by the brave and tireless men and women of the Resistance.

There was a noisy party at the Huisman's the night before Deane-Drummond and Whitmill said their farewells, which succeeded in waking the neighbours. A timely reminder that there were German soldiers billeted in the houses nearby who might not appreciate the English songs, soon quietened the party down. At dawn the following morning the pair were taken to Oud Reemst, about 6 km east of Ede. They travelled in an ancient charcoal-powered Red Cross lorry, hidden beneath a heap of sacks on the floor. Guided on foot through the woods they soon came to a clearing with a long barn in the centre and were amazed to see about 30 paratroopers standing outside the barn checking equipment and brewing up. Inside the barn were a further 20 members of the Division resting. There was a supply of British uniforms and weapons, dropped by the RAF and smuggled in to the woods by the Resistance and the Major and Whitmill quickly changed out of their civilian clothes and back in to British uniform. The party of around 50 armed and uniformed British had now to travel almost 20 km on a roundabout journey, in broad daylight, to a second location close to the river and that night's crossing point.

This next stage of the journey was to be in three antiquated lorries, miraculously produced by the resourceful Resistance. The escapees lay on the floor of the lorries, two layers deep and covered with dusty potato sacks, throughout the long and uncomfortable journey. Twice they came upon German checkpoints but each time, as the Paras prepared themselves for a battle, they were waved straight through. They passed through Ede at dusk, then continued along a minor road through Bennekom and eventually Renkum where the stiff and bruised passengers parted company with their transport. As they were clambering down from the trucks with much English cursing, a group of German soldiers on bicycles came pedalling down the lane towards them, ringing their bells in warning. The British stood to one side, weapons clutched tightly with safety catches off, but the cyclists rode past without a second look.

The escapees stumbled through the forest behind their guides to another rendezvous where they joined a second group which included Brigadier Lathbury. The party now numbered about 150. It was around 9.30pm when the party set off on foot for the final 3 miles to the river led by Major Digby Tatham-Warter of the 2nd Battalion and Dutch guides. The first couple of miles were through the woods and the men walked in pairs to reduce the length of the column. They were under the strictest orders to remain as quiet as possible as they passed dangerously close to German positions, but despite these dire warnings Major Tatham-Warter thought that it sounded like ... "a herd of stampeding elephants" ... behind him. As the men grew more tired from their first real exertion for almost a month they stumbled in to each other, tripped over tree roots and fell in to ditches in the darkness. At the edge of the woods the escapees parted company with their Dutch guides and, with much hand-shaking and whispered thanks, the men from the Resistance slipped quietly back in to the shelter of the woods.

It was now 11pm and they were less than half a mile from the river. The route was across open fields under the guns of the forward German outposts. The Paras crawled through the grass, hugging the ground and using the little cover afforded by drainage ditches until a gentle slope took them down to the river's edge. Now the men could regroup as a fighting formation with strong patrols on either flank and up ahead in case of contact with the enemy. Reaching the river bank the party turned westwards and followed the river towards the pre-arranged RV with the boats. The silence was suddenly shattered by the chatter of machine guns ahead. The advance patrol returned fire and, surprisingly, the enemy broke off the engagement and silence returned.

On the stroke of midnight a stream of red tracer was fired across the river from the south bank to signal the crossing point. The recognition signal was returned from the north by Tatham-Warter flashing a shielded torch and the anxious Paras settled down to await the boats. After an agonising wait of half an hour there was no sign of them. Had they arrived at the right place? What had happened to the boats? Had the operation been compromised by a traitor? It would be another half an hour before the next tracer signal was fired, and in the meantime the men were in a totally exposed position should the enemy choose to put up a flare.

A Canadian Officer, Leo Heaps, who had dropped at Arnhem, been captured then escaped to join up with 2nd Army south of the river, was one of the organisers of Operation Pegasus. He had crossed to the north bank to meet the evaders and suddenly appeared out of the darkness to confront a startled, but very relieved Tatham-Warter. Heaps led the line of men along the bank to the correct crossing point south west of Renkum where assault boats manned by Sappers were waiting. It took three crossings for the boats to take Wally Whitmill and the rest of the party to the safety of the south bank. Once ashore white tape guided them to a farmhouse and the HQ of an American Parachute Battalion. Copious quantities of tea and buns were provided before an assortment of Jeeps and trucks took them back down the line to Nijmegen and a reception with something a little stronger than tea to drink and a welcome bed. After a thorough questioning and debrief the evaders were flown back to England to begin a well-earned leave with their families.

After Operation Pegasus there were still over 100 Paras remaining in hiding north of the river. A second evacuation, Pegasus 2, was planned for the 17th November to bring back 160 Officers and men. Sadly, the operation proved a total disaster and many of the evaders and brave Resistance fighters were killed when they were intercepted by enemy patrols. The amount of publicity given to Pegasus 1 had obviously alerted the Germans and this time they were ready.

A group of happy Airlanding Brigade survivors at Nijmegen after the evacuation of the Oosterbeek Perimeter.

Lcpl Wally Whitmill, the evader.

Harry Wilce reads his first English newspaper in Stalag 11B

Stalag 11B at Fallingbostel.

RSMs John Lord and Bill Kibble with a smiling group of ex-POW's shortly after the camp was liberated.

Dennis Riley soon after arriving at Stalag 11B.

Cpl Roy Tyler and Lcpl Clements with female Norweigan admirer in 1945.

CHAPTER 9

PRISON CAMPS AND ESCAPES

I used to dream about a huge bar of chocolate dipped in a tin of Nestles Milk

(Cpl 'Jock' Mills during the 350 mile Long March in 1945)

For many of the eager paratroopers who landed at Arnhem the next few days were to bring a number of vivid shocks in to their young lives:

1. The opposition they faced was far stronger than they had been let to believe,
2. They were wounded, and
3. They became a prisoner of war.

These were traumatic shocks to the system of men who, only a few days previously had been enjoying the carefree freedom of an English summer. Men who, after 5 years of global war, could see an end to the terrible conflict and a brighter future with their wives and loved ones. And then suddenly, they found themselves in a foreign country, tired, hungry, dirty and exhausted, terribly wounded or their position overrun by the enemy as the last of the ammunition was spent and their pals lay dead around them. Their immediate fear was of being shot out of hand by their captors. Hadn't Hitler himself referred to them as 'Gangsters'? But their fears were completely unfounded and Lt. Colonel Frost was to remark later that the SS who finally re-took the bridge were, "Kind, chivalrous and even comforting". Similar reactions were experienced by many of the 2 Officers, 2 Senior NCOs and 47 Junior Provost NCOs who were captured.

On the morning following the withdrawal from the Oosterbeek Perimeter almost 2,000 wounded members of the Division were left behind to be cared for by 200 Medics and Army Chaplains. In addition, a further 300 men remained on the north bank of the river when the rescue mission ceased at dawn. Individuals and pockets of troops had been captured throughout the previous 8 days as units were surrounded or became cut-off from relief. In total the Germans claimed 6,450 prisoners taken, wounded and not. A small number were able to escape during the confusion in the first few hours or days following their capture and went into hiding, either to await the arrival of 2nd Army or to cross the river later with Operation Pegasus. For the majority of the prisoners however there followed months of captivity and deprivation in a German POW Camp.

When daylight came on Tuesday the 26th, the Senior Medical Officer, Colonel G.M.Warrack, toured the Perimeter and Div. HQ collecting together all the wounded. A number of ambulances and lorries took these men the 30 miles to Apeldoorn where a British Military Hospital had been established with the full co-operation of the Germans. As Colonel Warrack later reported:

In my opinion, a great deal of help was given to the Airborne Medical Services because the Germans were so impressed with the splendid fighting qualities of the men who had been wounded, or by their gallantry in the recent battle.

Captain Jock Gray, the Officer Commanding the Provost Company, who had been so badly wounded during the withdrawal on the previous night, was one of those wounded taken to Apeldoorn for emergency treatment. Sadly he was to die there of his wounds and is now buried in the Airborne Cemetery at Oosterbeek with 5 other members of his Company.

Wounded were gathered at Apeldoorn from the Casualty Stations and First Aid Posts hastily established during the battle, from Kate ter Horst's neat house beside the old Church at Oosterbeek, from the Schoonoord and Vreewyk Hotels and the St. Elizabeth Hospital. When their captors decided that they were in a fit condition to travel the wounded were sent by train across the border in to Germany, usually crammed into cattle trucks, sometimes for a journey that took many agonising days. On the 26th September 500 walking wounded made the first of those terrible journeys from Apeldoorn to a waiting Prison Camp.

Corporal Harold Bennett, who had unsuccessfully tried to join up with his Section at the Arnhem police Station, and who had been badly wounded in the defence of Div. HQ, was one of those taken from the St. Elizabeth Hospital:

> *The first few days there were chaotic and in the confusion quite a few of the walking wounded arranged to slip away. After a while we were moved over the border and put in to the hospital ward of a civil prison. I remember the nurses, who were all Nuns, coming round with small gifts for the wounded on some particular occasion. From there they moved us by train on what seemed an endless journey to Stalag 11B near Fallingbostel. I met up with some other members of the Company there and we were all able to exchange news of what had happened to all our mates. I remember one young lad there who had managed to lose a tooth so he modelled himself a false one out of a toothbrush handle. My own biggest worry was having an arm or a leg amputated. The wounds were still playing me up and I had seen the pitiful state of some of the other prisoners with the bones sticking out from their wounds after amputation. There appeared to be very little in the way of medical supplies, and only very thin paper bandages. Fortunately, it didn't come to that for me.*
>
> *That winter was pretty cold and there was no heating in the camp. If we wanted a fire we had to search around for wood to burn on it, usually the planks off our beds. The food situation was equally as bad and I can remember being permanently hungry. That Christmas I won a raffle and the prize was a piece of horse meat and a Christmas pudding which was made of bread crumbs and bits of fat.*
>
> *Most evenings we heard the 9 o'clock news from London on an illicit radio which someone had built from bits taken from aircraft wreckage which had been cleared by POWs*

under German supervision. On Easter Sunday 1945 I was in the hospital ward in a critical condition. In addition to the problems with my wounds I was suffering from malnutrition and pneumonia. I remember Captain Bonham-Carter came in and presented all the patients with an egg for Easter. We had no idea where, or how, he managed to get hold of them, but they certainly tasted good.

A few days before my birthday in April the camp was liberated by our advancing armies and, after a thorough delousing session and the issue of some decent clothing, I was flown back to England and into a Medical Centre in Hemel Hempstead. I had a couple of years in an orthopaedic hospital near Mansfield and they managed to save my arm and leg. While I was in hospital there a letter arrived, written on a scrap of brown paper, which I had written in hospital at Apeldoorn to try and let my wife know where I was. The Dutch nurse I gave it to was in the Resistance and had channelled the letter, via Geneva, to my home address.

Lcpl John 'Claude' Raine from Bexleyheath in Kent, was captured along with other members of his 4th Parachute Brigade Provost Section on the 20th September fighting alongside Brigade HQ:

After we were captured we were marched to Apeldoorn and later put onto a train for Germany. We were given two small pieces of bread for the journey which turned out to be five days long. We were starving. I was sent to Stalag 8C at Sagan and I've never been as cold as I was that winter. Just after Christmas I got dysentery and became very weak. Early in the New Year we were all paraded and told that we were going to march off to another Camp. Just a couple or three days march away we were told. I was in the Camp hospital at the time but all the patients were declared 'Fit To March', and off we went. After the three days they just kept on marching us. My feet were playing up and I kept dropping back and suffering a good few hidings from the German guards.

Stalag 8C was close to the Polish border and in the path of the advancing Russian Army. Prisoner of War Camps in their path were hastily abandoned by the guards, taking their prisoners with them as hostages or insurance against an unknown future. The war was rapidly reaching its conclusion and Europe was in turmoil. Towns and villages lay ravaged and in ruins, armies advanced or retreated across borders, millions of homeless people were on the move as they sought to escape the violence and destruction sweeping over the land. Roads were choked with shuffling lines of humanity pushing, pulling or carrying their meagre possessions on whatever form of transport was available; hand carts, prams, old bicycles, wheel barrows or, for the fortunate ones, a farm cart pulled by an emaciated ox or horse. Whatever means of transport the refugees had it was piled high with their treasured belongings and the family struggled along beside it. To this pitiful westward migration was added the marching prisoners. John Raine continues:

> *It was obvious that very many of the prisoners were ill. We were cold, tired, starving and with totally inadequate clothing against the wintry conditions. Me and the Signaller, who had lost an eye at Arnhem, managed to slip away from the march without being seen and headed back in the direction we had come from. We fell in with a group of French prisoners who had a couple of elderly German guards with them. The French had a handcart piled with food which they had pinched from somewhere, but they refused to give us any. Then one of the guards took some and passed it to us. We stayed with the French for a while, all the time heading away from the Russians.*
>
> *The Germans were terrified of the Russians and what atrocities they might commit.*
>
> *We were really lousy by this time, still wearing the same clothes we had left England in weeks before, and we hadn't been able to get a wash for days. I got a dose of dysentery again and was getting steadily weaker as we plodded on hour after hour. We passed through a town and I was taken into a building, a Dance Hall I think, and lain on some straw on the floor along with hundreds of others. They were all in a*

bad way and many of them died while I was there. They kept me there for about a week and I spent my time either killing lice on my clothing, or hobbling to the toilet. This was an open trench outside in full view of everyone in the town.

One day, anyone who could walk was marched to the station and crammed into cattle wagons. There was a small hole in the corner of the truck just big enough to empty a mess tin through and this was the only toilet facilities we had. After about four days and hundreds of air raid warnings, during which the guards would jump off the train and disappear, we arrived at Stalag 11B near Fallingbostel. We were in a hell of a state by this time but I was found by some of my mates from the old Company who looked after me. I had my first wash and shave for weeks and was given clean trousers, shirt and boots. It was luxury – but I still had my lice.

The next day I was interviewed by the Camp Leader RSM J.C. Lord of the 3rd Parachute Battalion. He questioned me about the march and I gave him a list of all those I could remember in Stalag 8C. Our paths never crossed again but I often wondered if I gave him some of my lice as well.

Not long afterwards we were liberated. I gorged myself on white bread, oatmeal, sugar, jam and anything else I could get my hands on. I made myself so ill I though I was going to die, but I was free at last and on my way home.

Corporal Jock Mills was in the same 4th Brigade Section as 'Claude' Raine and had been shot through the arm. Captured shortly after his Section Sergeant, Austin Roberts, was killed, he was taken to Apeldoorn and from there to Stalag 8C. His memories begin with the train journey into Germany:

We were on that train for four days, crammed into those trucks and standing up the whole way. If we all squeezed together there was just enough room for a couple of the wounded lads to lie down. There was no water to drink, and just a tiny window high up in one corner of the truck. It started to rain so we smashed the window and pushed a piece of cardboard through, then passed the cardboard around so that we could suck it and get the water out. There must have been about 50 or 60 of us crammed into that truck.

They took us first to a Transit Camp, Stalag 12A at Limburg. There were about 500 of us crammed into a big marquee, without bedding so we sat on the muddy floor back to back to try and get a bit of sleep. After a day or two they moved us on to Sagan.

At first it wasn't too bad with only three of us sharing a loaf of bread. Then another 500 or so prisoners arrived and the loaf had to be shared between twelve. About Christmas all our bedding was taken from us as a reprisal because the Camp Commandant said that German prisoners in Egypt had to sleep on the sand.

At the start of 1945 the Camp was emptied and we set off on what became known as The Long March. By the end we had marched, or rather staggered, over 350 miles. My memories of that terrible period are all jumbled together. I just remember the cold and the constant hunger. On one occasion we were told that we had to spend the night in the open. The guards drew two parallel lines in the snow and told us to lie down between them. Anyone who moved out from between the lines would be seen as escaping and would be shot. Another night we were billeted in a farm and after we had been locked in the large barn some of the men went hunting for food. They found some wheat in the bottom of a barrel and ate it, but the wheat had been soaked in poison to kill the rats and, sadly, a couple of the lads died.

Our numbers were gradually depleted as prisoners dropped out or died of their wounds and the bitter cold. One night we stopped at a ruined castle and at least we had a roof over our heads. We were marched into the courtyard then up some stone steps into a sort of tower. The room was large and empty and they locked us inside. We looked through a window and saw a walled vegetable garden down below. Somebody had a length of rope and a couple of the lads volunteered to go down and get some of the vegetables for us as we were all starving. We lowered them down and they got the veg' and we hauled it back into the room. We were then so weak that we hadn't the strength to pull the two lads back up. The German guards caught them down in the garden and they were clubbed to death.

Then it was back on the road again. Shuffling along, trying to keep up with the rest, trying to keep warm and, most of all, trying to find something to eat. There was a big, fat German Officer with us who used to ride alongside on a little white pony and always feeding his face. **We** *had to make do with anything we could find in the fields. Blokes used to fantasise about all kinds of food and their favourite meals, describing every mouthful in great detail until you could stand it no longer and shouted at them to shut up. I used to dream about a huge bar of chocolate dipped in a tin of Nestles milk. Lovely! The march ended at Stalag 9B north of Frankfurt where we were put into wooden huts. This was luxury. We couldn't believe it. One morning we woke up and all the horrible guards had gone leaving some old timers, like Home Guards, to look after us. Soon afterwards the Americans arrived and we were released. I weighed four and a half stone by then.*

Jock's wife, Sally, has vivid memories of his homecoming and of the few days afterwards:

In October 1944 I had received a letter from the Provost Company saying that Jock was listed as 'Missing'. Then some time later a man in a shop at Mexborough where we were living told me that he had heard on the radio that Jock had been captured and was a prisoner. That was the first I knew that he was still alive.

Later I was told that he had been liberated and that I was to meet him off a certain train at Mexborough Station. When the train arrived I couldn't see him amongst the soldiers getting off. I eventually found him in a compartment filled with other ex-prisoners, all of them too weak to move. One of the poor men had already died. We had not been told to expect anything like this and it was terrible to see the condition Jock was in.

When we got home I sent for the Doctor right away. When he arrived he was so shaken that he sent for the local newspapers to take photos of Jock. He looked like something out of Belsen. I was told that he would probably die, and that the best thing would be to put him in hospital. I said that if he was going to die then he would die at home having made the effort to get back here.

We had saved up all our Ration Coupons and invited some of the family round for a slap-up meal. Jock had Ham and Eggs and the rest of us had Fish and Chips. Jock ate all his own food up, then proceeded to eat everyone else's. If he was going to die it would be on a full stomach.

After that it was a long, slow recovery and he was in and out of hospital for many, many months.

Lcpl Paddy Breen, one of the General's motor cycle escort, was wounded on the 25th as he made his way through the woods behind the Hartenstein Hotel towards the river. An explosion had severely damaged his ears and eyes and by morning he too was a prisoner. Following treatment at various hospitals in Germany he was sent to a POW Camp near Mulhausen. Within a few days he was moved again and spent Christmas 1944 working in some salt mines. There were a number of other British POWs there who had been in captivity since Dunkirk, four and a half years previously.

The following February all the prisoners left the mines to walk westwards. In fact, they were to join the route of The Long March at Weimar and complete the final 145 miles of that horrific journey. Paddy Breen had other ideas:

There were about 300 of us on the march including a lot of Canadians, and the idea seemed to be to keep us away from the approaching US Forces. Then it was rumoured that the Russians were near and the guards got quite jittery. At night we were usually herded into barns and the length of the breaks we had gave us a good idea how close the Americans were. One day they marched us through a large town which didn't appear to have any bomb damage at all, then as we left the town and climbed a hill we looked back to see the place getting a right plastering from some dive bombers. I'm ashamed to admit it now, but at the time it gave our morale a right lift. One night we were marched into a farmyard about 6pm to rest up for the night. In the middle of the yard was a big dung heap and on it was a rotting cow's hide. We were so hungry that we tried to pick the bits of meat off the hide. About 9pm the guards started shouting that we were moving again so that we reckoned that the Yanks couldn't be all that far away. I'd palled up with a French Canadian soldier named Paul and the two of us managed to hide in a hay loft when the rest of the prisoners left. We covered ourselves with hay to wait until either it was safe to move or the Americans arrived.

As soon as all the prisoners and guards had gone the barn underneath the hay loft was occupied by a group of German soldiers who rested up for a few hours. As they moved on so another lot would take their place. This went on all through the night and for the following day and night too. All the time we lay perfectly still not daring to make any sort of movement or noise in case we were discovered.

After the last lot of Gerries had gone we heard the sound of tanks. Paul moved a tile off the roof and peered through, then he shouted down to me ... "Americanos" ... We jumped down from the loft and rushed outside. At first all I could see were Germans, then I realised that the Yanks had made the Germans ride on the front of their tanks in case there was an attack.

After being interrogated by the Americans, then fed and clothed, we were flown to Brussels and from there back home in time for VE Day.

'Junior' Stubbs had been captured with the remains of the 4th Brigade Provost Section only two days after landing. Taken initially to the POW Staging Camp at Limburg for documentation, he was soon moved deeper in to Germany to Stalag 4B at Muhlberg. There he was to meet up again with two other members of the Company,

Lcpls 'Bat' Barlow and Monty Page who had been captured during the Airborne assault on Sicily. It was Monty Page who forged 'Juniors' Pay Book promoting him to Corporal so that he wouldn't have to go out on work parties for the Germans. Page was also 'on the run' from the enemy inside the Camp. He had covered for an escaped RAF prisoner by exchanging names and the escape had later been discovered. Monty wasn't on the ration strength of the Camp and, consequently, he had to hide each time there was a Roll Call. Stubbs describes their eventual liberation:

The Camp was liberated by the Cossacks and then the Russians moved the main body of the prisoners out of the Camp and marched them off in the direction of Russia. There were about 6 or 7 Airborne Military Policemen and we were left behind as Camp Guards. We were to accompany the sick when they were thought fit enough to be taken off towards Russia too. When it was time for them to go the Senior British Medical Officer advised we Policemen to head for the American lines. Four of us from the Company, Bernard Phillips, Bernard Quinn, 'Bob' Hope and myself set off towards the Yanks. We had quite a few brushes with the Russians and on one occasion they pinched my bike, which was a pity because I'd only just nicked it from an empty house.

We called at a house looking for food and ended up staying with them for almost a week. There was an elderly couple, their son, three daughters and a daughter-in-law. All their husbands were missing on the Russian front. Anyway, they fed us like lords and in turn we stocked their larder by going out at nights and doing a spot of looting on nearby farms. We also managed to 'acquire' a big, fat pig, a sheep and a load of vegetables by telling the owners that the Russians were going to confiscate them anyway. We left the family and crossed over in to the American lines and within a couple of days we were flown home by Lancaster Bomber then sent home on a glorious leave.

Lance Corporal Stan Reast had been captured on the night of the evacuation from the Perimeter, and the following morning had buried his Officer and one of his mates. A few days later, along with many other prisoners, he was marched with hands raised through the streets of Arnhem to the Railway Station. It was a humiliating experience but the soldiers tried to make light of the situation by singing and whistling. Many of the civilians who watched the sad procession were wary of approaching the prisoners or of showing any sign of comfort, fearful of German reprisals. There was, however, some official help for the prisoners from the Dutch people. Stan Reast explains:

> *The marvellous Dutch people had set up a feeding station for us. It was only a watery potato soup, but it was hot and we were cold and starving. It tasted wonderful.*

After the grim 4 day rail journey packed with 50-odd other prisoners in a cattle truck, he arrived at Limburg Staging Camp:

> *There we were documented and registered with the Red Cross. The only shelter was a large tent and we had to try to sleep on the floor. It was crowded and absolute chaos at night in the dark with people stumbling about trying to get to the toilets. These consisted of about 30 fat drainpipes stuck upright in the ground with their tops protruding. We had to sit on the tops of the pipes for toilets. Someone warned us to be careful because the toilets sometimes 'blew-back'.*
>
> *I had my birthday in that Camp. What a birthday. The only good thing about it was that I was able to send off a card to let my wife know what had happened to me.*
>
> *After a week or so I was stuck into a cattle truck again for another crowded, uncomfortable journey of three or four days, this time to Stalag 4B at Muhlberg. There we were not made to work and consequently the time dragged. There were quite a few different nationalities in the Camp, but the French seemed to be the most organised. Many of them had been there since the start of the war and they even had their own hairdresser. A couple of fags would get you a decent haircut.*
>
> *Like a lot of the lads there I was lousy and had no clean underwear to change into. I managed to get hold of a couple*

of flour bags and one of the French tailors cut me a pair of drawers. A bit rough but they were clean.

The toilet facilities in the Camp were pretty primitive and consisted of either a large bucket in the middle of each hut, or toilets where you could shovel the smelly contents out of the back. One of the punishments, if you were caught pinching anything off another prisoner, was to be pushed down into the toilet. Either that or the thief was made to Run the Gauntlet between lines of fellow prisoners armed with sticks. Stealing off your mates was one of the worst crimes you could commit and the guilty person would receive a right beating. Dividing out the rations also caused a problem. We would get a small box of potatoes between six of us. These would be laid out on the table in rows of six with the biggest spuds at the top, then the next biggest and so on. Then we would cut the cards for who had first choice of the rows. We also had one small brown or black loaf between the six of us which would be very carefully sliced up, with everybody wanting the crust, and again we would cut the cards for who had first pick. We didn't have a knife so I sharpened up one half of my POW Identity tag and this served as a knife. Talking about bread, there was a large 'Shit Wagon' in use around the Camp. This was a big tank on wheels and every few days 20 or 30 prisoners would have to drag the full wagon out in the field nearby and let all the contents of the wagon run out. Extra bread from somewhere would be smuggled back in to the Camp wrapped in sacking and hidden inside the empty tank. I never fancied any of that bread.

Towards the end of April 1945 all the German guards left the Camp in a hurry and within a couple of hours the Russians arrived and set up machine guns at all the Camp entrances to keep us in. Joe Unsworth and I had been together in the Camp all the time. We quickly provided ourselves with a couple of sleeping bags and even a bike. I gave the bike to a female Russian Officer in exchange for six big tubes of soft cheese. They kept me and Joe going for quite a while.

*One night Joe and I went through a hole in the fence and started heading in the direction of the American forces. Every time we passed houses with German civilians in they would beg us to stay the night. They knew that if **we** were in the house then they wouldn't be bothered by the Russians. For some of the civilians it was too late and the Russians had already been through helping themselves to the contents of the farms and loading their plunder onto the farm carts before moving on.*

```
"FALLINGBOSTEL"  XMAS 1944

8.15 AM      TEA. EGG. BACON. MASH.
             B. BUTTER  MARMALADE.

10.30 AM     TEA. BISCUIT - BUTTER.

11.30 AM     PEAS - POTATOES.

3.46 PM      SALMON SANDWICHES - TEA.

6 PM         PEA SOUP. THICK.
             FRIED POTATOES.
             FRIED ONIONS.
             STEAK? (HORSE)!!
             XMAS PUDDING & CREAM.
             BISCUITS - CHEESE.
             TEA, LAGER BEER, MILKY COCOA.

             "KAMMER STAFF" i.e. 4 LADS +
             1½ CANADIAN RED + PARCELS.

                  STALAG. XIB.
```

Did Harry Wilce really eat horsemeat?

> *Soon after we got out of the Camp we met up with a group of Paras. They had got hold of a small cart from somewhere and we piled all our kit onto it, plus a Red Cross food parcel we had pinched. I'd never had a whole Red Cross parcel to myself all the time I had been a prisoner. I'd had a sixth of one, or even a quarter, but never a full one. We pulled that truck for about 4 days, all the time heading towards the Americans. One day we came to a bridge over a river. On the other side of the river were the Americans, but the bridge was guarded by a huge Russian soldier and he was not letting anyone cross. We retraced our steps and waited until we had gathered together about 20 or 30 ex-prisoners, then formed up in to three ranks. One chap produced a battered Officer style cap, put this on and marched us off towards the bridge. As we got closer he had us all marching to attention, then brought us to a crashing halt in front of the Russian, before handing him some papers. God knows what the papers were, but the Russian didn't know either. He just saluted and waved us over the bridge.*
>
> *After that it was just a case of handing ourselves over to the Yanks who overwhelmed us with their usual hospitality then sent us back to Brussels. There it was de-lousing, issue of fresh uniforms, de-briefing and a night out on the town before we flew back to the UK.*

Lcpl Jock Keddie, together with his Section officer, Lt. Wilf Morley, had been captured at the Arnhem bridge on the 21st following the defiant and magnificent stand by the Paras. They were both unaware that the remainder of the Section, less than half a mile away at the Police Station, were already in captivity.

> *They marched us away from the bridge and down a side street, then made us all sit in the gutter. There were guards walking up and down all the time, but occasionally one of them would drop you a cigarette and whisper something like ... "Me Lithuanian, not German. Me Friend".*
>
> *They marched us off in the direction of Germany and after a while we were halted and moved into a big barn. The*

SS turned up and all our boots were removed. A few hours later the guards returned and flung some old German Army boots at us in exchange for our good old Para boots. The ones we got were ill-fitting and full of nails. Not the ideal things for marching in. Then it was back onto the road and marching again. Convoys of German Army lorries passed us heading for Germany and laden with loot they had taken from Arnhem, loads of tools, sewing machines, linen, and furniture. There was all sorts on those wagons. They made room for us and we were taken to a Railway Station and crammed in to cattle trucks. After 2 or 3 days of being shunted in and out of sidings every time a German military train was on the line, we eventually arrived at Stalag 11B at Fallingbostel.

Stalag 11B was built in 1939 and when the first members of the 1st Airborne Division arrived the camp already housed a large number of Poles, Russians, French, Belgians, Yugoslavs and Dutch, plus a handful of British POWs. The Airborne prisoners were allocated huts previously occupied by the Russians and had first to set about repairing blocked and broken toilets and ridding the huts of an army of lice. Winter was fast approaching and the prisoners were ill-prepared. Warm clothing and blankets, food, fuel for heating and basic medical supplies were in desperately short supply. By early December the Camp held over 4,500 British prisoners, practically all of them Airborne, including 800 wounded brought in by hospital train from the Arnhem area. Not surprisingly the prisoners were totally dispirited and demoralised as they were herded through the Stalag gates in to the lice-ridden huts. Their future looked very bleak indeed.

Amongst the first of the Airborne prisoners to arrive at Stalag 11B was RSM John 'J-C' Lord of 3 Para, who had been wounded in the right arm and captured when trying to reach the Arnhem bridge. Originally from the Grenadier Guards, he was to be reunited with a pre-war fellow Grenadier in the Camp, RSM Bill Kibble CMP, who had been wounded and captured at the Hartenstein Hotel. RSM Lord was to become a legend amongst all those who were POWs at Fallingbostel, although at first there were many who did not appreciate his methods. As the Senior British Officer in the Camp he assumed responsibility for the welfare and behaviour of the prisoners inside the British Compound, and set about improving conditions as far as was humanly possible.

Huts planned to hold 200 prisoners were eventually crammed with 450 and it was imperative that they were kept clean, aired and that the sanitary facilities were improved. He encouraged the prisoners to exercise regularly by walking around the Compound, organised soccer matches and concerts and got the Germans to allow forage parties of prisoners to leave the camp to collect wood for fuel. RSM Lord led by example and ex-POWs still recall his immaculate turnout under those difficult conditions. Somehow he would appear with highly polished boots, his trousers retained their knife-edge crease with the old Guardsman's trick of laying them between two boards and sleeping on them, and the German soap came in handy for whitening his belt.

The frequent Roll Calls held by the Germans were a shambles with the prisoners, including the many sick and wounded, being made to stand outside in the freezing cold sometimes for hours until the headcount was completed to the German's satisfaction. John Lord took over, parading the thousands of POWs before formally handing the parade over to the German guards. Hearing the British words of command and seeing that, if only for the Roll Call, the British were in command, did wonders for the men's morale. The RSM even acquired a bugle from the Germans and introduced daily bugle calls throughout the British Compound. But perhaps his biggest contribution to the morale of the men was the dignity and soldierly bearing he brought to the many sad military funerals held inside the Camp. The filthy handcart provided by the Germans to carry the body would be thoroughly scrubbed and polished beforehand, a homemade Union Jack was produced with which to drape the coffin, and a bearer party was formed of the tallest and smartest of the prisoners. Finally, the bugler sounded the Last Post as the body was laid to rest. By his example and leadership, in the true manner of the best of the British Warrant Officers, he gave the prisoners back their pride in themselves, in their uniform, and in their country.

> **Kriegsgefangenenpost**
>
> **Postkarte** — 53 Geprüft Stalag XI B
>
> An: MR & MRS J RILEY
> 25. HAWKSTONE. AVE.
> GREENSIDE LANE
> DROYLESDEN
> MANCHESTER
> LANCS
> ENGLAND
>
> Absender: L/CPL. DENNIS RILEY.
> Gefangenennummer: 117975.
> Lager-Bezeichnung: M.-Stammlager XI B

> **Kriegsgefangenenlager** — Datum: Nov 5 1944
>
> Dear Elsie & Jim, Hope you recieve this OK. I am beginning to settle down here a little now, my wound is healing up fine too. I haven't seen Tom, but I heard he was also wounded, so he was probably taken prisoner, as the hospitals we were in were all captured. I will write if I get more news. Love to the children. Cheerio. Dennis xx

Mail from the POW's was eagerly awaited.

Jock Keddie recalls his meeting with RSM Lord when he arrived at Stalag 11B:

> We were paraded in lines when we got to the Camp and this RSM approached. His arm was in a sling, but other than that he was immaculate. Creases in his trousers, shiny boots, the lot. As he walked up and down the lines he was followed by a soldier who carried a cardboard box. He gave the first man a piece of soap, the next man a razor, and the third a

shaving brush. Then the RSM said, .. "Be back here in half an hour washed and shaved" .. That changed my whole view of the situation. That made me a British soldier again. Just looking at him, tall and erect, just as though he was on guard at Buckingham Palace.

Lcpl Harry Wilce, another of the Policemen captured on the night of the evacuation, also found himself in Stalag 11B within a few days.

*We were accommodated in long huts with tiered bunks. At the end of our hut there was a small room where RSM Lord and RSM Bill Kibble bunked. I remember one of the funerals RSM Lord organised. The Funeral Party was drilled by the RSM, gaiters and belts were cleaned and brasses polished by using dirt and stones. Boots were even polished somehow. The burial ground was quite a way from the Camp and the whole party slow marched there. It really put the Germans to shame and made **us** feel an awful lot better.*

There was a large hut there holding long-term POWs who had been captured in the early days of the war. They were all on Working Parties away from the main Camp and seemed so well organised with regular Red Cross parcels, parcels from home and parcels sent from other friendly countries. One chap had been there that long that he had almost finished a Law Degree correspondence course.

Jock Keddie was placed on one of the 'Arbiet Kommandoes', (Working Parties), away from Stalag 11B. With him went Lcpls 'Canada' Young and 'Stinger' Inns.

They marched us off one day to this Hermann Goring works where there were lots of different nationalities working in and around this big factory. They put us to work digging deep trenches for pipes of some sort. We were at it from about 8 in the morning until late at night. There were also a lot of lads there who had been captured at Dunkirk 4 years before. After that we worked on laying a railway branch line into the factory. There was ourselves and a Russian crew who had a bit of a hard time from the German guards. We were laying sleepers, pretty hard work, and all we had to eat was a piece of bread and some potatoes each day. We lived off that for months. Then the Red Cross parcels started to arrive, one between two, and we gorged ourselves on Spam, Corned Beef, and coffee. We also got hold of some sugar beet off the Russians. This would be put in a can, covered with sand and left in the fire when we went to work. When we came back in the evening we'd take off the shell and the beet was lovely and brown and filled you up a treat. The skins we passed to the Jews or Political Prisoners we saw every day.

My 'uniform' at this time consisted of a long, royal blue, French Colonial overcoat, some old trousers and a jacket, then a peaked cap with 3 or 4 different colours around it. This odd outfit helped when we managed to get hold of some bread coupons and I was able to go in to the civilian's canteen and get a ration of extra bread without being recognised.

Another time we pinched some onions from an allotment shed beside the railway and smuggled them in to Camp under my long greatcoat. Half of them we gave to the Camp Doctor because he said they were good for the blood and some of the prisoners needed them. The others we swapped with a New Zealander for some tobacco. We had nothing to eat the onions with anyway.

In the Spring of 1945 we were told to pack up because we were moving out within a couple of hours. We could hear heavy gunfire in the distance and the Germans were obviously getting worried. 'Stinger' Inns had a plan to hide down a manhole in the Camp when we all left and he asked me if I would make sure the manhole cover was put back on when he was down there. 'Canada' and I said we would stay together and stick it out. They marched us all out about 3 o'clock in the afternoon and headed for the North East of Germany. They marched us all through the night and then about 6 the next morning we rested in a big barn. We must have been marching too fast because the elderly guards didn't come in for a rest until a couple of hours after us. There was only the Commandant of the Camp, who was riding on a horse and cart, who managed to keep up with us. When they marched us off again it was only for a couple of hours before we rested again in another farm building. The guards said that we would be staying there overnight.

The next morning there was a big American tank at the gate with its gun covering the farmyard. The Commandant went up to the tank, to surrender I suppose, but the Second in Command of the Camp walked up behind him and shot him right through the back of the head. The tank's machine gun fired a quick burst and almost cut the second German in two. We went back in to the barn and disarmed all the guards.

The Yanks gave us something to eat then told us to walk back down the road in the direction of their troops. On the way we teamed up with two South Staffs from the Airlanding Brigade. We got hold of a couple of chickens and some veg' and started to prepare a big stew over a fire. We were looking forward to a right good feast when an American soldier came up and said ... "Can't you understand, you're winning the war"... With that he took us to the nearest house, kicked open the door and said ... "Get in there and help yourself"... That sort of attitude didn't appeal to us, but we were starving and soon found ourselves something to eat.

While we were in the house a German civilian came in and took us to stay with him. I think he just wanted protection in case the Russians arrived. We agreed to stay with him for a few days, with the South Staffs lads in the house next door. Behind the houses hidden away in this little village, was a small factory where they were said to have manufactured the poisonous gas for the gas chambers.

Within a few days the village was filled with escaped prisoners all waiting to be told what to do next. The Russians arrived, all heavily armed and looking very fierce, but didn't bother us when we said that we were British escaped prisoners. They just went through every farmyard killing all the animals and taking them away for food. Eventually we *were instructed to make our way to an airport where we were fed, clothed and deloused before they flew us back to England.*

Bill 'Stinger' Inns of the 4th Parachute Brigade Provost Section had been forced to surrender when he was wounded twice as he tried to shelter behind a small tree close to the Wolfheze Railway Station. He tells what happened next:

The two Germans manning the Spandau machine gun shouted for me to walk towards them with my hands in the air. They searched me and took my Para boots, giving me a pair of wooden ones in exchange. They also took my watch, fountain pen, cigarette case and all my money. I was taken to a German First Aid Post and from there to a large house which was full of British wounded all waiting for treatment. I was bleeding pretty badly and someone came to look at my wounds. They removed all my bloodstained clothing and then started probing around in the wound on my elbow. No anaesthetic or anything, just probing and prodding around. I don't think they ever did find the bullet. They just put a dressing on it and left it. When I stood up I must have passed out because I came to on a stretcher with two German soldiers carrying me up two or three flights of stairs. They tried to get the stretcher through a doorway but were having a bit of a struggle as I weighed around 15 stones at the time. Anyway, I climbed off the stretcher and walked the rest of the way. We were kept in this house for a couple of days with our only food coming from some Dutch people who provided us with soup.

When we were considered fit enough to be moved we were marched to the Railway Station and loaded onto coaches with wooden slatted seats. We sat there for ages before a British Medical Officer came in to the carriage, took one look at the state we were all in, then set on the German guards. He gave them a right telling off and consequently we were all moved in to a better carriage with a Polish Medical Orderly to look after us.

After a few days we arrived at Stalag 11B. My arm was in a sling so the only useful thing I could do was to collect firewood for the fire in the hut. Soon afterwards I was moved out to a Work Party at Hallendorf with some others of our Provost Company. I was still wearing my wooden boots, stuffed with straw because I had no socks. I also managed to get hold of a woman's chemise from somewhere, miles too big for me but winter was coming and anything would do to keep me warm. I also acquired a jacket and other bits of clothing.

At Hallendorf we were put to work building a huge air raid shelter, but there wasn't much I could do with my arm. I tried carrying the bags of cement but one of the German guards said ..."Nein, you are wounded" ... I think he was the only decent guard I met. He put me back gathering bits of wood for the fire. I remember whenever there was an air raid the Russian prisoners would all run and stand next to an Englishman. They thought that they wouldn't get killed that way.

As the war progressed and the Allies advanced deeper into Germany there were quite a few escapes from the Camp. Some got away with it, and others were quickly caught and brought back to spend a few days in the 'Cooler'. We heard on the grapevine that the Russians were pretty close and that prisoners were being marched out of the Camps ahead of the Russian advance. We also heard that some American prisoners had been marched for hundreds of miles and arrived at their destination more dead than alive. I knew that I had to get away and head towards the advancing British. I just didn't fancy being part of one of those long marches. Then the order came for us to pack our belongings, and I knew that this was it.

I'd seen a manhole just behind our hut and I decided that I would hide down there during the night and stay there until all the guards and POWs had left the Camp. I joined up with an RASC lad and another British prisoner, then collected some bits of food including a packet of Horlicks and a spoon. We climbed down the manhole when it was dark and Jock Keddie made sure that the lid was firmly back in place after we were down. It was a very narrow, brick-lined shaft with a metal ladder bolted in to the brickwork on one side. It was very cold down there as we each managed to get a foot on the ladder and just hung there in the pitch darkness. I was in the middle of the three and we hung there for hours listening to the noises in the Camp above us as all the prisoners were paraded ready to march off. Then it all went quiet.

We stayed where we were for another couple of hours to make sure that everyone had left, then, when we worked out that it must be dark outside, we decided it was time to come out. The chap above me pushed on the iron lid but he couldn't budge it. The lid was too thick and heavy and was firmly fixed in the hole. No matter how hard he tried it just wouldn't shift, either he hadn't got the strength, or it was wedged too tight. I squeezed my way past the chap above so that I could have a go. I tried to get two hands on the lid but I couldn't because I still had to hang onto the ladder. We started to panic just a little, thinking that we could be stuck down there forever now that the Camp was empty. All the rest of our mates and the guards had left and nobody would miss us. What a thought. It was inky blackness and freezing cold and what bit of strength we still had was slowly draining away. Then the smallest of the three of us, I think his name was Smith, somehow struggled to the top of the ladder, got both his feet firmly on a rung, then put his back against the lid and pushed as hard as he could. The lid slowly lifted upwards and the night air rushed in.

Twenty four hours previously the area around the camp had been open ground, but now an enemy anti-aircraft unit had positioned their guns there and the place was crawling with Germans. As we silently crept away from the Camp the air raid alert was sounded and the gun crews stood to their guns. We could see tiny lights glowing in the night from the instruments on the guns as we crawled through the grass between them. After what seemed hours, but was probably only 5 or 10 minutes, we were through the guns and on the far side of the field. We spent the rest of the night moving as far away from the Camp as possible, walking along narrow lanes and through fields, crossing streams and giving a wide berth to houses and farms. It was bitterly cold and none of us was best dressed for being out in the open that night, but the knowledge that we were heading towards freedom kept us moving.

We rested for a while in a large haystack, rubbing our soaking boots with the hay to dry them off. Then we pushed on again wanting to get as far away as possible before daybreak. We were walking through a thick mist when we heard what sounded like a squad of troops coming in our direction. We dived through a hedge in to a field and could make out the shape of mounds of something dotted around, so we each rolled behind one for cover. It was only when the troops had passed that we realised we had been lying behind heaps of fresh, smelly horse manure.

As it started to get light we went into a wood to hole up for the day. We lay down in the bushes and covered ourselves with leaves and twigs to try and get some sleep. We had only been there a few minutes when the ground was shaken by an almighty bang. Peering through the bushes we saw that we had settled down about 10 yards from a German gun position. We crept away as quickly and quietly as we could and headed back in the direction we had come from to an isolated barn we had passed during the night.

*By this time we were pretty exhausted. The barn was dry and warm and I spread my big overcoat over the three of us on the floor. We had a mouthful of milk and Horlicks each then fell in to a deep sleep. Some time later I heard German voices outside the barn, but for some reason they never came inside. We just lay there under the greatcoat, wondering what was going to happen next. Then one of the Germans came in carrying a Panzerfaust, a sort of Rocket Launcher. After speaking to the others outside he walked over to where we were lying on the floor, took one look at the ancient greatcoat and asked of we were French soldiers. I said that we were. He said that he wasn't German, he was Polish. I replied that **we** weren't French but English. With that he handed around his cigarettes, propped his weapon in the* *corner, and walked outside. We still didn't quite know what to make of it. Then a few minutes later we heard the soldiers outside shouting that American tanks were coming up the road. I jumped up and ran outside waving a bit of dirty rag towards the tanks. Someone fired and the round whistled by too close for comfort so I dodged back in to the barn and exchanged the second-hand German jacket I was wearing for Smithy's British Battledress blouse before I ventured outside again. Sure enough they were American tanks. I shouted up to the tank Commander that we were escaped British POWs and once he was satisfied that we were genuine out came a large bottle of brandy to celebrate. The Yanks wanted to take the four Germans as their prisoners, but I said ... "No they're **our** prisoners" ... Besides the Gerries were keen to stay with us. That's how I came to capture four Germans armed only with a spoon.*

We made our way to the American HQ, warmed by the swig of brandy, and reported to an Officer there explaining who we were and where we had come from. While we were still standing in the open a Jeep pulled up with a German Officer sitting smugly in the passenger seat. He was wearing a beautiful pair of highly polished boots. I thought of the boots the Germans had taken off me at Arnhem, so I relieved him of his boots and gave him my old wooden ones which I had had to wear all through the winter. The American Officer objected to this and said that we shouldn't treat the enemy in that way. I soon put him right in no uncertain terms.

*We were passed back down the line making our way slowly towards Brussels, hitching lifts on trucks returning to the rear, until we reached the British Sector. By the reception we were given, in contrast to the way we had been treated by the Americans, you'd have thought **we** were the enemy. Interrogation, questioning, more interrogation. I don't think they believed us when I said that we were escaped POWs, because we must have looked a right trio in our mixture of dress. As soon as we could we crossed back over in to the American Sector where we were fed again, deloused and flown back to England.*

At Fallingbostel RSM Bill Kibble was responsible for the control and distribution of Red Cross food parcels, and this allowed him to leave the Camp to visit the local Railway Station to collect the parcels. Such visits were always under armed guard, but they gave the RSM the opportunity to get to know the guards. RSM Lord wanted to ensure that every British prisoner in the Camp, regardless of rank, received an equal share of the parcels, and that the men saw that this was the case. Food parcels containing certain items of nutritious value were passed to the sick and wounded. In the Spring of 1945, with the Allied Armies advancing from the East and West, the supply of Red Cross parcels ceased completely. More prisoners were brought into the Camp and the possibility of starvation became a real problem. The POW's Committee learned that there was a stock of parcels at the docks in Lubeck, but that the Germans were unable to distribute them because of the damage caused to their railways and roads. A Swiss Red Cross Representative visiting the Camp confirmed this to Bill Kibble and that only transport was needed to get the parcels to the prisoners. Using his contacts with the German guards, and a small amount of precious coffee as a bribe, Bill Kibble somehow managed to persuade the Germans to provide the transport and guards to allow him to travel to Lubeck to collect the life-saving food parcels. The 3 or 4 day journey was fraught with dangers, false papers and the 'greasing' of many palms with coffee, Spam and tins of bully beef, but the resulting issue of parcels within Stalag11B undoubtedly saved many lives. (The full account of the journey is recounted in Richard Alford's excellent biography of John Lord, *'To Revel in God's Sunshine'*.)

One of the first veterans with whom we made contact was ex-Lance Corporal Jack Coates who had been captured at the main Arnhem Police Station. Jack produced for us a personal diary he had kept in his Police Notebook, commencing on the day he flew out of Lincolnshire and running through his time at the Police Station and in captivity to January 1945 when the paper ran out. The diary had not seen the light of day for almost 50 years and it is regrettable the restriction on space will not permit us to print the diary in full here. Jack describes the diary as ... "Pretty boring reading as it is all about food and fags" ... On the contrary, we found it a fascinating document and, with Jack's permission, copies of it together with all our other research papers can be studied at the Hartenstein Museum (Oosterbeek), The Airborne Forces Museum, and the Royal Military Police Museum.

The typed recollections of Jack Coates run to over 50 pages, almost a book on their own, and whilst it is frustrating it is necessary that we condense his excellent reminiscences to the following extracts. We are sure Jack will have understood.

On the day following his capture at the Police Station he was marched, in a long column of prisoners, about 30 km to Zutphen. There they spent the night in a large warehouse before being packed into the usual trucks for the journey in to Germany. Four and a half days later, without water and only a few morsels of bread to eat, they arrived at the Reception Camp of Stalag 12A at Limburg. After two weeks at 12A, during which time Jack was put to work clearing bomb damage from the streets, he joined a large party who were to spend another 5 days travelling across Germany to Stalag 4B near Leipzig. This was a well established Camp with British Senior NCOs in charge and even boasted a shop, theatre, market and church. After only a brief stay at 4B he was moved again, this time on an Arbiet Kommando (Work Party), in the city of Halle. There they were based at Stalag 4D which also housed a number of French prisoners. Jack Coates continues:

> There were about 200 prisoners in our British compound, self-sufficient under the command of a tiny Feldwebel and his troop of mainly elderly guards, most of whom seemed thoroughly fed-up with the war. Fred Wilkinson from Number 1 Section and I remained together, sharing upper and lower bunks in the corner of the room and sharing Red Cross parcels whenever they came along. I can only remember one occasion when each man received a full parcel, usually they were shared between two, three or even more. All the prisoners in our room were Airborne men, and out of a total of 18 most were from the Airlanding Brigade, mainly South Staffs.
>
> Food, or the lack of it, was the consideration uppermost in everyone's mind. Apart from how much longer would the war last, our biggest problems from day to day were how

much food would the Germans give us, and when would the next Red Cross parcels be issued? The Germans seemed to give us as much as they could spare, which wasn't a lot because they were tightly rationed themselves, and Red Cross parcels must have been way down on their list of priorities when they were fighting with their backs to the wall.

Our work in Halle consisted of tunnelling below ground on the outskirts of the city, somewhere near the River Saale. We were digging out what we assumed to be an air raid shelter, for it was used as such by the local population when the regular air raids took place. It was an extensive network of tunnels but whether it **was** a shelter, or whether it was intended for some other purpose we never did find out. It was already in existence when we arrived, and it was far from completed when the war ended. During the last few months of the war Halle became a target for the Allied Air Forces with waves of Flying Fortresses by day and the RAF by night bombing the area. We shared the shelters with the German civilians when they took cover and wondered if we were going to meet our ends at the hands of our own side.

We prisoners worked in 8 hour shifts around the clock and were taken daily back and forth across the city by tramcar. Going to work and travelling around in public did something to relieve the tedium of POW life. Our 'work' was rewarded by payment in small sums of Reichsmarks and we were able to make petty purchases in the local shops, such as pencils and notepaper, certainly nothing in the food line. Our relationship with the local population was somewhat ambivalent. They came and shared our shelter when the alarm sounded and we mingled with them quite naturally. Many were young women and children and some of the women would surreptitiously slip cigarettes to our men. Naturally, any young men or German soldiers who took shelter had a different outlook and they were more inclined to sneer and jeer at us.

In the final weeks of the war the bombing of Halle and district intensified, and eventually we were switched from our work in the tunnels to the task of burying the dead. Much to our annoyance we were told that we would have to work on Good Friday 1945. Afterwards we were relieved that we **had** been in the town because during the raids that day our Camp had been badly damaged and a number of prisoners, mainly French, had been killed. The Camp was quite badly damaged with fences down and the place wide open. There was nothing to prevent a mass escape, except the fact that in the chaos and confusion there was nowhere to go, and we had no idea how close, or how far, were the liberating armies. A few of our fellows did make off, but were soon brought back. The countryside was crawling with Hitler Jugend and other trigger-happy Nazi fanatics and at that stage there was certainly safety in numbers.

It was soon afterwards, as the Allied Armies advanced from the West, that the Germans marched us out of the Camp towards the East. During the march I teamed up with Jack Koop, a Londoner who had been in one of the Para Battalions and a room mate in the Halle Camp. Jack kept us fed in those final days. He was a dab hand at turning out pancakes from potato flour and anything else we could get hold of. On one memorable occasion he got into a hen run and caught a bird and it wasn't long before we were feasting on roast chicken.

We moved at a leisurely pace across the farmland and open country of Eastern Germany, living off the land, scrounging and bartering as we went along, until we reached the hamlet of Galen. It was here that a small group of American tanks caught up with us and for us the war really **was** over. We were showered with American rations and cigarettes and entertained by the Yanks. One of them took us to the local Gasthof where he called upon the landlord to produce beer and other drinks. The poor landlord protested that he had nothing to give away, whereupon the Yank drew his .45 in a most threatening manner and forced the unfortunate German in to his cellar where he managed to find a bottle of something. Through the Americans we were quickly flown home to England and I was still on leave when VE Day dawned.

It has been necessary to select just a few sample extracts from Jack's diary to give an insight in to the privations and suffering endured by the thousands of POWs.

MONDAY 25 SEPTEMBER 1944
11am. Detrain after 4 days crammed in to cattle truck with 50 others. Weak and hungry. Deloused. Searched. Bathed. Bowl of soup in evening. Sleeping on floor in tent with 1 blanket.

SATURDAY 30 SEPTEMBER 1944
Working in morning. Received first Red Cross parcel. Contents; Tin Corned Beef. Tin Margarine. Tin Butter. Tin Jam. Tin Marmalade. Tin Spam. 100 Cigarettes. Box Sugar. Box of Dried Prunes. Tin Dried Milk. Box Biscuits. Tin Meat Paste. Tin Peanut Butter. Box Cheese. Orange Juice Tablets. 2 Bars of Chocolate.
Sharing parcel with Fred Wilkinson (CMP). Ate too much and spent very bad night. Three trips to lavatory with diarrhoea and sickness.

TUESDAY 10 OCTOBER 1944
On the move again. Been on the train since last Friday. 50 of us to a cattle truck. Been in captivity three weeks today. No food today except what we had in reserve, also some bread traded from a German with soap. Thinking about home a lot.

FRIDAY 13 OCTOBER 1944
Managed to have a shave. First for a week. Bought box of small potatoes for 15 cigarettes so will have a good feed today. There are 250 in our hut all trying to use the one fire to cook our food on. Food takes up 75% of our thought and time, plus home and the course of the war, of which we know very little.

MONDAY 16 OCTOBER 1944
Had a much needed hair trim, the first for 6 weeks. Cab,

(Sgt. Cab Callaway) gave me my last at Barkeston. He is dead now, shot when the rest of us were captured at the Police Station. Learned that we are all moving out on Kommando (Work Party).

FRIDAY 20 OCTOBER 1944

Now at Halle working on some kind of tunnelling. The tale that it is an air raid shelter is hard to swallow. Still bad with diarrhoea.

MONDAY 23 OCTOBER 1944

Reveille at 0430. Parade at 0500 then taken by tram to work at the shelters. Drew Red Cross parcel. These were from Argentina and are OK. Don't know how we would survive without the parcels. Notices posted around the Camp warning that escaping is no longer regarded as a 'sport' and that any POW doing so will, in all probability, be shot.

SUNDAY 29 OCTOBER 1944

Dinner today raw red cabbage, mash and alleged meat. I never got any of the latter. As usual this evening is 'Scoff Evening' with everyone wading in to the Red Cross parcels. Just six weeks ago we were entering Arnhem. Spasmodic machine gun fire was my baptism, everything ran so smoothly. It looked like being a very successful Op. According to all reports it was – but not for us!

TUESDAY 21 NOVEMBER 1944

Sick again and got another two days in the Sick Room. These rations are having their effect. Can't wash my clothes and they are filthy. Can hardly keep my body clean. Rumour of Jerry soap issue this week. Big air raid nearby this morning bags of flack going up. I got knocked about by the sentry who used his rifle butt to get us in to the shelters.

MONDAY 11 DECEMBER 1944

Every bone in my body is showing through and it looks as though I am wasting away. Stomach not back to normal yet by any means. More cases of diphtheria and we are confined to Camp in quarantine.

CHRISTMAS DAY 1944
One more day nearer home. No work today. The Guard came in at 7am to get us out of bed. We told him it was Christmas, but he kept coming back to try and get us up. Eventually got out of bed at 10am. Too cold. No fire as we are saving the small amount of coal. Breakfast two rounds of toast with sardines, piece of chocolate, lump of cheese and a brew. Mid-day and an air raid warning. Even today the RAF won't give the Hun any peace. Into the shelters with bags of community singing of patriotic songs. Dinner at 2pm, better than we had expected under the circumstances. Mashed potatoes, swede, turnip and meat with carrot gravy. (I added some corned beef to this). Then macaroni saved from the past fortnight by the cooks, and cooked well. To this I added sugar, milk and stewed prunes, courtesy of the Red Cross. With dinner we had some beer which was pretty good stuff.

NEW YEAR'S EVE 1944
15 weeks. I wonder where Harry Greenwood is now, and if he remembers our last New Year's Eve. We caught the train from Barnard Castle to Bishop Auckland and then walked back getting in at Reveille. Those were the days. It's been freezing like the devil all week and snowed last night. Swapped a shirt for two loaves but soon scoffed up. Air raid warning tonight and had to turn out though I tried to dodge the sentry and remain in the hut.

The diary ends in the middle of January 1945 with the comment from Jack Coates .. "This is the end of the notebook and the diary. It was not possible to obtain another. Sorry."
Throughout his time as a POW, in the various Camps, on the terrible rail journeys, and on the Work Party at Halle, Jack had one mate alongside him. He was Fred Wilkinson who had been a member of the same Number 1 Section captured at the Police

Station. Although they lived and worked together for so many long months, in overcrowded huts with little chance of privacy, Jack was most surprised to learn from us during the research for this book that Fred had also kept a detailed diary during that time. It tells of the same conditions during that winter, the same shortage of food and the almost total reliance on the irregular Red Cross parcels.

To continue with Fred's diary where Jack's ended:

26 JANUARY 1945
I have been in hospital for 6 days with diphtheria. Two boys have already died. There are also 4 Danes in the same room. We hear that the Russians are in Germany so it shouldn't be long now before the war is over.

7 FEBRUARY 1945
Still in hospital with diphtheria. Last night I slept on the floor as they brought a Yank in and there was no bed for him. A great many of the Yanks are suffering from frostbite. They were on a train carrying prisoners for 10 days over Christmas and had no food or blankets.

15 FEBRUARY 1945
We have had 9 air raids in the past 48 hours. Tomorrow I will have been in hospital for 28 days. Yesterday we were peeling Swedes for the soup so I had a good feed off them raw. Two more air raids in the night.

23 FEBRUARY 1945
This has been a good day. This morning a Frenchman in the hospital gave me his bread, then at dinner I had two bowls of soup and a bowl of porridge. This afternoon the Russian and I had to go and shift some spuds so we filled our pockets with them and tonight we cooked them on the fire.

31 MARCH 1945
Went through one of the worst experiences of my life. There was an air raid and a bomb hit our shelter. I was buried

under all the rubble for an hour. There were 120 of us in the shelter and around 50 were killed. It was awful.

13 APRIL 1945

This morning at 3am the prisoners started on a long march away from Halle. We could hear the artillery in the distance as we left. For three days we walked all over the countryside with only raw spuds to eat. On the fourth day myself and two Yanks slipped away from the march. We changed direction and headed West. We were fired on by German troops on a number of occasions but did not get hit. Our nerves were at breaking point and every little noise made us hit the deck. At one point we must have crawled for almost a mile.

On the 18th, shortly after 6.30 in the morning, we saw dozens of tanks heading towards us. We just slung our kit away and ran for cover. A couple of the tanks opened up on us with machine guns, but we were dead beat. We just lay there sweating. When the tanks got a bit closer one of the Yanks peered through the grass and saw the white star on them. We leapt up and ran towards them waving our arms and yelling at them not to shoot. They gave us food and cigarettes, then told us which way to walk towards safety.

Two hours later we met up with the Infantry and it was all over...

WE WERE SAFE.

CHAPTER 10

THE SEABORNE ECHELON

There was a rumour that British Jeeps had been seen crossing the Arnhem Bridge and that Liberty passes were being issued to go in to Arnhem

(John Hamblett with the Seaborne Provost Section.)

The Seaborne Echelon, mentioned in Chapter 3, was commanded by Major R.D. Sellon KOSB and had an approximate strength of 84 Officers, 2180 Other Ranks, and 1100 assorted vehicles. The Provost party was commanded by Lt. F. McPherson Royal Artillery and was made up of two Sections. Support Section under the Sgt N. Phillips and Cpl Fielding with 13 Lcpls formed part of the main convoy with the Company's transport and stores. The transport consisted of 8 Jeeps and trailers, 4 x 15 cwt trucks and 1x3 tonner with a number of motor cycles either being ridden or carried as a cargo. Number 6 Section under Sgt F. Barnett with Cpls John Hamblett and E.A. Armstrong plus 12 Lcpls were responsible for route signing and escort duties for the convoy.

After the dawn farewells had been said at Stubton, both to the other members of the Company and to the ladies of the Land Army next door, the Provost vehicles joined the main convoy at Stamford and headed for the docks in London. Hamblett takes up the story:

The convoy set off about 6.30 on the Sunday morning, August the 13th and took all day to reach the Transit Camps near the docks. The Camps were large cinder covered areas full of tents and not the most welcoming of places. We settled in, not knowing how long we were going to spend there, but hoping that it wouldn't be too long. The surrounding area appeared to have received a right plastering from enemy bombers and Flying Bombs and none of us fancied spending any longer in the area than was necessary.

Everyone was issued with an inflatable lifebelt, Expeditionary Force money and a ration pack, then we settled down for the night. Early the following morning the vehicles were called forward and were loaded onto Liberty ships at the east and West India Docks, and at the Victoria and Albert Docks. Loading of the vehicles and personnel took all day and it wasn't until about 7 o'clock that evening that we finally set sail down the Thames.

The crossing to France was uneventful but lengthy and it was late afternoon the following day before we anchored off the Normandy invasion beaches. We lay at anchor throughout the night of 16/17th August and the following morning the whole convoy could be seen lying off shore. It really was a tremendous sight with dozens of smaller Landing Craft buzzing around like a swarm of bees, and hundreds of large barrage balloons overhead to protect against enemy aircraft. In fact, there was an air attack during the day but the beach anti-aircraft fire kept them at a safe distance. Early on Thursday morning Landing Craft came alongside each of the larger ships and vehicles were hoisted out of the holds on to the LCTs (Landing Craft Tanks), to be ferried ashore. The drivers and passengers had to scramble down nets in to the LCTs which was rather a precarious operation as the ships rose and fell with the swell. Eventually we were ashore and the CMP Beach NCOs directed the vehicles to 'Goldsmith' Transit Camp at St. Croix sur Mer, inland from Gold Beach. Once the whole of the Echelon vehicles were together we moved to a concentration area close by where we bivouacked in a large orchard adjoining a US Army unit.

During this period we suffered our only casualty when Lcpl Fitzpatrick was involved in a traffic accident whilst on convoy duty. He received a fractured pelvis and was left behind with the Field Ambulance.

We remained in this area for the next couple of weeks during which time, if we were not busy on the maintenance of vehicles and equipment, we were escorting groups of German prisoners to the POW Cages or patrolling nearby Bayeux which was open to Allied troops for recreation. As usual on such occasions the problem was one of keeping the troops occupied lest boredom set in. The Army Education Corps organised local language classes and produced 'PEGASUS', a daily news sheet to keep us informed of the progress of the war. Film shows were organised in a large tent but rainwater coming in through a hole in the tent ruined the film after the first showing, so that was that.

For the first few days in France tentage was still in short supply and it was a case of finding shelter where we could, even sleeping underneath our vehicles. One evening in August we were awoken from our slumbers by the guard and men appeared from their resting places under trees, lorries, in Jeeps and any other sheltered place, to witness the barrage which signalled the start of the Falais Gap breakout by the great Allied Armies. The skyline was a blaze of lights of all colours and the sound of the crashing explosions was deafening. Something was happening at long last.

At the end of August we were warned to be ready to move within 48 hours. No reason was given but the excitement rose as we thought that we were going to get involved in the war at last. On the 2nd of September information was received that the Airborne Division were to drop within the following 24 hours in the vicinity of Lille, and the Seaborne Echelon moved off at 5.30 that morning to link up with them. We drove through what was left of the outskirts of Caen and there was total devastation. Houses and buildings were wrecked and the streets were piled with rubble. Dead Germans were lying beside the road with piles of abandoned equipment and wrecked vehicles everywhere you looked. But I shall always remember the dreadful smell of the long-dead cattle. It was unbearable.

We followed a route north west for some 130 miles before halting for the night at the town of Cisors to the north west of Paris. Headquarters was set up in a Chateau which had only recently been vacated by a German Medical unit, and the vehicles found cover in the surrounding woods. The following morning we were told that the airborne drop, Operation Linnett, had been cancelled. However, once petrol had been found for our hundreds of thirsty vehicles, we were off again, this time another 40/50 miles to a harbour area between Crevecoeur and Conty just south of Amiens.

Scattered parties of dispirited enemy were rounded up in the area and escorted by Provost to the nearest POW Cage. We remained south of Amiens for the next few days before the news came through that Brussels had been liberated and that we would be moving up there just as soon as it was safe enough to do so. At 1pm on the 6th of September the convoy was on the road again spending the night dispersed beside the Amiens/Albert road. The following day was routine as normal as we refuelled and escorted the long column of vehicles a further 100 miles to a harbour area a few miles south of Brussels. The welcome given by the people of Brussels to the liberating troops had been overwhelming and any military vehicles were still finding it difficult to force a way through the crowded streets. Consequently, our move on the morning of the 8th bypassed the city and we halted in the town of Louvaine a few miles to the east. The Provost Section were billeted in a school, the first time for days, if not weeks, that we had a proper roof over our heads.

While the Echelon Commander anxiously awaited news of any proposed Operation by the Airborne element of the Division, the troops in the convoy enjoyed a much needed rest. No move from their present location was expected in the immediate future and the men used the time to maintain and repair their vehicles and to indulge in a spot of fraternisation with the locals. Brussels was still Out of Bounds to the Seaborne Element, although Mobile Patrols by Number 6 Section had been sent in by the Section Commander, Lt. McPherson. On the 11th September it was announced that an ENSA Show would be given in the grounds of Div. HQ at Terban Monastery that day, and that the entertainers would be the well known Flannagan and Allen, Florence Desmond and Kay Cavendish. ENSA was the acronym for Entertainments National Service Association, but was more commonly known to the troops as, Every Night Something Awful. On the 12th permission was given for 50% of the soldiers to visit Brussels on each of the following three days between 3pm and 11pm. Transport was provided and Provost were tasked by HQ with providing patrols in Brussels and Louvain, "To check turnout, behaviour and passes."

At 8pm on Wednesday 13th, just 4 days before the great air armada was to descend on Holland, the Div. Commander, Major-General Urquhart, together with two senior members of his Staff, paid a flying visit to the Echelon. After breakfast the following morning the General broke the news of Operation Market-Garden to a hushed gathering of Echelon Group Commanders. This was the news that the men of the Seaborne Element had been eagerly awaiting since the Division had returned from North Africa 9 long month ago. At last, after so many false starts, 1st Airborne was being committed to the battle and there were many in the Seaborne convoy who cursed their luck at not being part of the great Airborne force. They were now anxious to press on, to link up with the ground forces as quickly as possible, to deliver the tons of stores and equipment they had carried all the way from Lincolnshire, and to become part of the great Division again for the final push in to the enemy's homeland.

At 7am the following morning the convoy was heading northwards again. It reached the village of Helchteren, about 20 km from the Belgian/Dutch frontier, around mid-day and waited to be called forward. The convoy was split in to 3 columns of vehicles in the order of priority they would be required, then for 5 long and frustrating days they sat and waited. On the 17th they heard the news over the radio of the Allied Airborne Operations taking place just a few dozen miles up the road in Holland. They watched in awe as the mass of aircraft and gliders passed overhead to deliver the American paratroopers to their objectives around Eindhoven. John Hamblett continues:

> *It had been a terrific morale booster to watch the Americans passing overhead, and the news was also encouraging about*

our own Division at Arnhem. There was a rumour that British Jeeps had been spotted crossing the Arnhem bridge and that Liberty passes were being issued to go in to Arnhem! Our convoy followed slowly northwards behind the Guards Armoured Division as it advanced. All around were the signs of the terrible carnage of war with shattered tanks and vehicles on both sides of the road. It was embarrassing to see the number of British tanks which had been knocked-out, and this was a warning of worse things to come. Our progress was agonisingly slow and our bumper-to-bumper convoy was frequently pulled off the road to allow more urgent vehicles to pass through.

By 6am on the morning of the 21st the main Column, including the HQ Group, was halted south of Eindhoven with it's tail just over the Dutch frontier. The other two columns of vehicles had been left behind at Helchteren. The main Column eventually moved forward again in the early evening heading through Eindhoven, St. Oedenrode and towards the bridge crossing the River Maas at Grave which had been captured by the American Airborne. The move was carried out without head or side light and met with a considerable amount of enemy activity and shelling from its flanks as the Column negotiated the narrow, congested road north of Eindhoven. John Hamblett again:

> *After leaving Eindhoven we made contact with the first of the American Parachute Divisions and evidence of the hasty German departure was everywhere. Equipment, clothing and arms were strewn all over the place. US artillery fired continuously from the fields on either side of the road and our progress became even slower as enemy attacks cut the road ahead of the convoy. On several occasions it was necessary to get the convoy off the road due to attacks and for the troops to dig in facing outwards to fend off any possible enemy infantry attacks.*

By the evening of the 23rd, Columns A and B were concentrated in a wooded area south of Nijmegan. The news from Arnhem, and in particular Oosterbeek, was not good and on the Saturday morning, the 25th, the Seaborne Echelon Commander, Major Sellon, attended a conference at Airborne Corps HQ to discuss the administration arrangements for the withdrawal of the survivors of the Division from Oosterbeek that night. It was estimated that about 2000 survivors would be received and for this purpose two large buildings were taken over in Nijmegen. One was a large school and the smaller a building known as the Pagoda to which the survivors would be taken to be documented, fed, re-clothed and given somewhere to sleep. Extra rations, rum, blankets, stretchers and clothing were obtained from 30 Corps and the two buildings made ready. Closer to the south bank of the River Rhine a tented Reception Area was prepared for the initial reception of the survivors before they were sent back down the road to Nijmegen. John Hamblett and his Section operated from the large school. He recalls that night:

> *We had the Jeeps and assisted in picking up the survivors as they came back over the river. They arrived in small groups throughout the night and were in a heck of a state. Many had a week's growth of beard and were covered in mud. Others had lost practically all of their clothing and came ashore to be wrapped in blankets or whatever other bits of clothing they could get hold of. As pals were spotted they hugged each other with relief at being safe and many a tear was shed that night. The survivors I saw appeared far from downhearted, but were clearly shocked at the outcome of the Operation and the fact that 2nd Army had failed to arrive in time as planned. Come daylight and the sorting out began. Rolls calls, listing of casualties, news of those taken prisoner. The survivors of the Provost Company were gathered together, only 13 of the 72 who took part had managed to cross the Rhine. The sight of this small group filled us all with great sorrow when the full impact of the disaster which had overtaken our Company was realised.*

Joe Smith was a Sergeant with 21 Independent Parachute Company and a long-time pal of John Hamblett's. He was one of the survivors and recalls their meeting on the south bank:

*My profound memory of John Hamblett was near Driel in the early morning during the withdrawal. I gathered a small posse of my Platoon, bedded them down for a couple of hours and then sent them on their way back down the line whilst I wandered around to see if there were any more when daylight broke. As I got to the Nijmegen road a Military Police Jeep roared up and ground to a halt beside me. In it was John looking, I thought, too bloody smart to be true. "Better hop in" ... he said ... "I'm looking for stragglers and things are starting to happen again". I climbed in beside him still very bemused by recent events, and let him do the talking as we raced down the road. I was safe and was grateful for his tact. There is a particular binding quality of friendship among men who have played together in the second row, slurped ale together after a game, **and** then belonged to the 1st Airborne Division.*

John Hamblett again:

When all the reporting, re-clothing and resting was completed a very sad and disappointed convoy, after travelling so far in good spirits, turned and was escorted back down the corridor by the Provost NCOs The survivors were taken to Brussels Airport from where they were flown back to England and a hero's welcome.

The Seaborne Element was routed through Ostend back to Tilbury Docks early in October. It had left England some 50 days previously in such high spirits to carry out whatever task it was called upon to perform. Much ground had been covered, but little seemed to have been achieved from a military point of view. We returned to our sadly depleted Company HQ at Stubton Hall and the very lonely and empty Nissen huts.

There was a second, smaller, Seaborne Element which included a half-Section of Provost. They left Tilbury Docks for France on the 22nd of September with the intention of joining the Airborne Element at Arnhem. They arrived off the Normandy beaches during the evening of the 23rd but, owing to the situation in and around Arnhem, remained on board the MV SAMHERN until the 29th awaiting instructions. Following news of the withdrawal of the Division the 2nd Seaborne Element returned to Tilbury without disembarking either vehicles or personnel.

CHAPTER 11

AFTER ARNHEM – NORWAY AND DENMARK

Here I bloody-well go again!

(Elderly German Officer, captured in Norway, who had been a POW in Nottingham during World War 1)

Sergeant 'Mac' McKnight was in charge of a small Rear Party which had remained behind at Stubton Hall after the Seaborne and Airborne Elements had left. Now he stood alone at the makeshift bar in the tiny Warrant Officer's and Sergeant's Mess. The news was that the survivors were on their way back from Holland and could be expected around 7.30 that evening. 'Mac' had lit a welcoming fire in the grate against the late September chill and made the Mess as warm and homely as he could. He thought the lads would like that. From somewhere he had rustled up a bottle of hard-to-get whisky and a couple of crates of beer. The door opened and Sergeant Dennis Yardley from Number 4 (Div. HQ) Section walked slowly in to the room. 'Mac' shook his hand warmly and then handed him a beer. He waited for the others to follow Dennis through the door. "Where's the rest of the lads?" he asked quietly. "There's only me Mac" Dennis replied. I'm the only one. All the rest have been killed or captured".

Eleven survivors, plus the Assistant Provost Marshal, Major Haig, and his Batman Lcpl 'Flash' Pulford, were all that reported back to Stubton that evening. The Company Rear Party, the Seaborne Element, plus one or two released from hospital, brought the total strength to 47. Three weeks before it had stood at 130. but as Cpl Roy Tyler was later to comment:

> *At the subsequent march through London and visit to Buckingham Palace our little unit marched with pride and humility.*

High on the list of priorities of those returning was a spot of home leave, then a re-issue of all the kit they had lost at Arnhem. The unit had then to be reinforced to its War Establishment and the call went out yet again for volunteers.

The Company was not to enjoy the hospitality of Stubton village, nor the company of the Land Army girls in the nearby Rectory, for much longer and there was many a tear shed when the Company moved to Harlaxton Hall near Grantham before Christmas. Built in the 1830s, this magnificent building was the home of the eccentric Mrs Violet Van der Elst when the Provost Company moved in. She abhorred all field sports and declared the grounds of her home ... 'A sanctuary for the birds and wild creatures' ... and would allow neither rabbits to be shot in the grounds nor even mice to be killed in the house. She was ardently opposed to capital punishment and would stage protests at any prison where a hanging was imminent, being frequently arrested for her troubles. Mrs Van der Elst had a library of over 3000 books dealing with the occult and the supernatural and regularly held séances in order to contact her deceased Belgian husband. Her fortune came from the manufacture of beauty preparation and the first brushless shaving cream, SHAVEX, which she first manufactured in her own kitchen. Into this environment of the rich and ornate building, and the presence of the eccentric and unpredictable Mrs Van der Elst, came the members of the Div. Provost Company.

With RSM Bill Kibble being a Prisoner of War, 'Mac' McKnight was promoted to fill the vacancy. He particularly remembers one of the lady's favourite spectator sports:

> *She stopped me one day and said ... "Oh Sergeant Major, could you get some of your men together, only I would like to see them run across the lawn". ... She said that she would give*

them a pound each and needless to say there were plenty of volunteers. I think there were about 30 of the men and she wanted them to strip to the waist and then run up and down the grassy bank at the side of the house. She would give them all a pound and me a tenner.

In the grounds of Harlaxton Hall grazed a herd of Shetland ponies, the leader of which appeared one morning painted maroon with Airborne wings in blue on it's flanks. There followed a frantic cleaning operation before the lady of the Manor caught sight of the beast. The culprit was not disclosed until many years later by Roy Tyler, - it was the REME 'Tiffy'. John Hamblett also remembers the ingratitude of the animals when, having been fed by the Policemen, would bite the backsides of their feeders. Could they be the origin of the Shetland pony mascot of the present-day Parachute Regiment?

Before our story progresses mention must be made of some of the Company's Arnhem veterans who aged and matured beyond their years during those 8 terrible days. Those who were fortunate to escape across the Rhine with the evacuation, and those captured and who were to spend many months in captivity, their fate uncertain from one day to the next. The released POWs were arriving back in England in April and early May 1945 as the Company was being readied for deployment with the Division in Norway and Denmark.

Corporal Jock Moir, who was evacuated together with his German prisoner, rejoined the Company at Stubton and was soon afterwards promoted to Sergeant. Lance Corporal 'Yoxy' Baker was one of only two members of Number 2 (4 Parachute Brigade) Provost Section who escaped with the evacuation. After leave he was posted out of the Airborne but remained with CMP and returned to Europe with his new Company until the end of the war. Dennis Fitzgerald of the Airlanding Brigade Section who was also on the evacuation remained with the Provost Company until the war ended when he transferred to the 1st Battalion of the Parachute Regiment and remained with them, at one stage as Provost Sergeant, until 1965.

Of the ex-POWs Stan Reast found himself, still with the CMP, posted to a factory in Scotland supervising a group of ladies packing

Army rations. Other similar jobs followed, marking time until he was demobbed and he could rejoin his wife in his beloved Devon. John 'Claude' Raine, after a mix-up with his Army Records, found that his transfer to CMP had never been recorded. Consequently, after leave, etc he was transferred to the RASC. Jack Coates spent some time with a Garrison Military Police Company in Hull. The duties of routine patrols, checking passes on the Railway Station and telling soldiers to button up their jackets or straighten their caps wasn't in Jack's nature and it wasn't very long before he was back with the Airborne Provost. There he remained until demobbed in early 1946. Others, including Cpl Jock Mills, Dennis Riley, Paddy Breen and Bill Inns were to require lengthy hospital treatment for their wounds before they could be either declared fit again for military service, or discharged. Harry Wilce appears to be alone in being sent to an Army Depot somewhere in the North of England where, along with many other returning POWs, he was introduced to basic military training. The intricacies of Foot Drill, the 36mm grenade and the Mk 1 Sten Gun. It goes without saying that this did not go down too well with Harry after all he had gone through, and he quickly got himself posted to 152 Provost Company HQ in Nottingham, just a few miles from his future wife, and saw out his remaining months 'pushing paper' in the Orderly Room.

On the 1st of May 1945 the Company was involved with the Division in Exercise Amber in Suffolk which was designed to test the many young and inexperienced reinforcements to the Division after Arnhem, and to ensure that the Division was ready for any future active Operation. Before the week was out the 'active Operation' became a distinct possibility when a Warning Order was received for Operation Apostle and the Exercise was terminated. The operation was to dispatch a strong force to Norway and Denmark to assist with the internal security and maintenance of law and order following the surrender of German forces there. By the 9th of May the Division was ready, its tasks being:

a) To maintain law and order.
b) To prevent sabotage of the important civil and military installations, dumps and airfields.
c) To maintain the security of operational airfields.

d) To ensure observance of the surrender terms by the Germans.

The Division was organised into 3 Brigades, each with its element of Support Troops, and was to occupy 3 lodgement areas, these being at Oslo, Stavangar and Kristiansand. At this stage it was not known whether the German troops would obey the orders from the German High Command for total surrender, or if the troops on the ground would oppose the Airborne landings. The first of the Div. troops flew into Norway on the 9th May to be followed over the next few days by Div. HQ and the attached troops flying from Tarrant Rushton, Rivenhall and Barkeston Heath. Others sailed from Scotland on the SS SAMINVER taking the unit vehicles. The Provost Company with Major Haig as APM, Captain McPherson the Officer Commanding and 'Mac' McKnight as the RSM, were located as follows:

OSLO FORCE	Company (less 2 Sections) and Company HQ
STAVANGAR FORCE	1 Section
KRISTIANSAND FORCE	1 Section

In Oslo the Provost Company occupied the Russelloken School with the NCOs carrying out routine security duties alongside the Norwegian Police. Sgt Jock Finlay and Cpl Roy Tyler were given a particularly delicate task as Roy Tyler explains:

We had been briefed to take the surrender of a Marine Battalion in Oslo so we sped off in our Jeep. The rejoicing crowds forced us to halt quite often during which time we kissed several babies, and lots of big sisters – ah! It was great being a liberator. A Norwegian Policeman jumped aboard and said that he would lead us to the Commandantura von Oslo where the Germans were busy destroying records. On arrival we found the Resistance in control with a small detachment on the pavement shaving the heads of women collaborators. Inside a terrific pre-incarceration party was in full swing with the Germans and their Women's Services. The whole atmosphere was unreal. Our Policeman eventu-

The newly promoted Sgt Jim Moir with a Norwegian Policeman.

In Denmark with captured German Kubelwagon.
L/R rear Lcpls E. Miller, W. Bazeley, E. Rodgers, Sgt J. Hannam, Lcpl J. Pendlebury. Front Lcpls W. Millar, H. Wilkins

Cpl Roy Tyler and Lcpl McDougall leave for the Naval Base at Horten, Norway.

CMP Motor Cycle Escort for King Haakon on his return to Norway.

ally led us to our destination which was surrounded by a cordon of Resistance. Sporadic firing had been going on for some time as the Marines would not hand over to civilians. Looking trustingly into the weapons protruding from the windows we drove up to the massive gates which opened and closed behind us with an air of finality. A grey haired Officer stepped from the crowd of armed men who surrounded us. His words amused me then, and do so now, ... "Good afternoon, Gentlemen. I am Captain Teschler. I am to conduct you to the Colonel. I was a prisoner in Nottingham for four years in the last war, and here I bloody well go again!" The Colonel said that he was not flattered at having to hand over to NCOs, but he was pleased we were English. Jock promptly informed him that he was as English as the Colonel was Jewish, and on this happy note we got down to business.

The newly promoted Jock Moir took his Section to Stavangar where they worked with the Civil Police rounding up all the Quislings or German sympathisers. He had only been there for a day when he received a telegram informing him that his son had been born and he flew home the next day. Lcpl Jim O'Sullivan was one of the post-Arnhem replacements and was in Jock Moir's Section at Stavangar. He remembers his main duties as being escorting high ranking Gestapo Officers to the town prison. One particular conversation with a group of prisoners has stuck in his memory as being particularly prophetic. When the prisoners were asked how they felt at losing the war, one of them replied ... "I'm not worried because in a few years time you will be asking us to fight with you against the Russians"."

In Oslo the Company provided four motor cycle outriders for Major General Urquhart's car when he led the triumphal march through the city. The NCOs were also on duty for the Crown Prince Olaf and King Haakon and the Royal Family when they returned to Norway. To assist with the security and patrol duties NCOs were attached from 243 HQ Provost Company, 70 Other Ranks and 20 War Dogs from 702 Company CMP (Vulnerable Points) and the 141st American Military Police Company. The tasks given to the Provost Company during those chaotic and uncertain days were many and varied, often of a nature which would normally have been dealt with by someone of a far higher rank. Roy Tyler describes one such duty:

> Lance Corporal McDougall and I were detailed to escort an Officer from the Prisoner of War Exchange Organisation to the Naval Base of Horten up the Oslo fjord. Near the town were four Camps full of Russian POWs, whom the local German Commandant refused to release until protection was provided for his men. Evidently two Airborne CMP NCOs were considered equal to the task.
>
> We travelled to Horten by boat and as we drew near to the docks we could see that the whole place was crowded, every crane and building had its quota of cheering spectators. A British Battalion had been requested and arrangements made for its reception, the Town Band, Fire Brigade, Scouts, Resistance Fighters, all were there and all ready for a triumphant march through the town. Anthems were played and speeches made, then we formed up. In the centre of the parade was a large gap, (for the absent Battalion), into which marched the Officer, a Black Watch Major in a kilt, then McDougall and I. We were laden with bunches of flowers, the band struck up, and off we went.
>
> The townspeople had prepared posies to throw at the expected Battalion. These had been made the day before and kept in water overnight. Sopping wet bunches of flowers rained down on us for the whole of the perambulations, and by the force with which some arrived it was obvious that our paucity in numbers was not popular in some quarters. By the time we appeared on the outside balcony of the Grand Hotel doing a 'Winston Churchill' we were soaked but happy.
>
> The following morning we were driven in charcoal burning Police cars to the first of the Russian Camps. The inmates were from Brigadier downwards and looked gaunt and lifeless, as did the German Guard of Honour awaiting us. Formalities were soon concluded. Ivan let out, armed. Fritz put in, unarmed. The Russian discipline was excellent and there were no incidents.

The local Resistance were using German prisoners to lift beach mines. A squad was given a particular area to clear and when their leader announced completion of the task they all had to link arms and march across it. If there were no explosions the party moved on to the next task. This proved a very effective system and after the first couple of days explosions were caused only through genuine oversight.

Shortly after our return to Oslo a youth led me to an underground store where the Germans had kept countless thousands of bottles of looted Champagne, Brandy and wines, and millions of cigarettes, pipes, lighters and other NAAFI type goods. After seeing that our Section did not go without I contacted the OC. **He** *arranged that the Company was not forgotten, then told the Assistant Provost Marshal at Division.* **He** *in turn ensured that the Officer's Mess was not overlooked, before passing what was left to the RASC for general issue.*

Lcpl Bill Millar was a member of Lt. McNinch's Section attached to 1st Parachute Brigade. The Brigade was tasked with a similar role in Denmark and duly flew in to Copenhagen early in May 1945. Bill Millar and a second Lcpl followed the rest of the Section 24 hours later. They were collected from the airport by Jeep and arrived at the unit's billets in town only to be informed that the Section was moving into the Koenig Frederick Hotel. Nobody knew exactly why, and nobody really cared, the chance of 5-star luxury doesn't come along that often in a soldier's career.

As Bill explains:

The time in the Hotel was great while it lasted especially being waited on at the table at meal times. The evening meal was out of this world. The tables were set as for VIPs with Danish and British flags on them on little stands. Every time we entered the Dining Room the other guests stood up and clapped us in. There was also a pianist playing during the meals and the only flaw in the arrangement was that we had to pay for our own drinks. Alas, all good things come to an end and eventually, when it appeared that there was some doubt as to who would foot the bill for our accommodation, we were politely asked to leave.

We then moved into an ex-German Army Barracks at the rear of Dagma House. This had been the German Army and Gestapo HQ and subsequently was taken over by our own Brigade as HQ together with Danish civilian staff. The Provost did Security Duty on the main entrance checking passes etc. We also worked with the Danish Police rounding up the remaining Germans in the area and escorting them to The Citadel in the centre of Copenhagen for searching and documentation. We then took batches of these prisoners down to the docks where they were held in large warehouses, documented again, then transported by boat back to Germany. The big occasion for us at this time was the visit of General Montgomery when we provided the escort for him through the city to our HQ, and from there to the Royal Palace where he was to be welcomed by the King of Denmark. The Military Police HQ was not all that far from the Carlsberg Brewery, as we soon discovered, and much to our delight we were informed that the beer was free provided that we returned the empty bottles and crates as soon as possible. Needless to say there was a regular Jeep and trailer shuttle running between Company HQ and the Brewery.

In early June 1945 the demise of the Company was on the cards when it was decided that NCOs with over a certain length of time still to serve in the Army would be transferred to the 6th Airborne Div. Provost Company who were about to leave for service in Palestine. Their places would be taken by NCOs due for demobilisation who would be posted in from the 6th Airborne. The first 22 Other Ranks arrived from the 6th on the 13th of June and the following day 28 NCOs from the 1st travelled in the opposite direction.

Many of the old stalwarts said farewell to the Company to join the 6th Airborne Division Provost Company at Bulford including Roy Tyler, Jock Moir, Peter Dale, Charlie Chaplin, Dave Lucia and Jim O'Sullivan, over 50 NCOs in total. The Company returned to England in September 1945, collected it's belongings from

Harlaxton Hall, and moved to Downton near Salisbury with the rest of the Division. The final act occurred on the 15th of November that year when the 1st Airborne Division, and with it the Provost Company was formally disbanded.

THE PEGASUS PATROL

ROLL OF HONOUR

They gave their lives whilst serving with the 1st Airborne Division Provost Company Corps of the Military Police:

LCPL. R. LAMB	TUNISIA	8th SEPTEMBER 1943
LT. V. WOODS	ITALY	21st DECEMBER 1943
LCPL. W.G. McBRIDE	ITALY	21st DECEMBER 1943
LCPL. T. COOKE	ITALY	22nd DECEMBER 1943
LCPL. E.J. HOOKWAY	ARNHEM	18th SEPTEMBER 1944
SGT. H.L. CALLAWAY	ARNHEM	19th SEPTEMBER 1944
SGT. A. ROBERTS	ARNHEM	20th SEPTEMBER 1944
LT. R.J. FALCK	ARNHEM	25th SEPTEMBER 1944
LCPL. P. JONES	ARNHEM	25th SEPTEMBER 1944
LCPL. J.T. NEWBY	ARNHEM	25th SEPTEMBER 1944
CAPT. W.B. GRAY	ARNHEM	29th SEPTEMBER 1944

THE AIRBORNE FORCES PRAYER

May the Defence of the Most High be around us and within us, in our going out and our coming in, in our rising up and in our going down, all our days and all our nights until the Dawn when the son of Righteousness shall arise with Healing in and His Wings for the Peoples of the World through Jesus Christ our Lord.

Amen

A SOLDIER'S WILL

The worldly wealth, the real estate, that such as I may own,
I leave my Mother should my fate have claimed me for its own.
Though gold and silver have I none, nor shares that could be sold,
I leave her, as her only son, a love worth more than gold.
Her way alone on earth must be, our mutual paths must sever,
Her courage all the world will see, our love will live forever.
To my sister all that I can leave, sweet memories of childhood days.
I hope, I pray, she will not grieve at this the parting of the ways.
I hope the pranks that once we played will bring to her a smile.
I hope that memories will aid her to make her life worthwhile.
And to my friends I leave the world, the flowers and trees I love so well.
Oh! May the beauty there unfurled outline all this war is hell.
To the sick and those in pain I leave the stars, the sun and moon.
I also leave to them the rain, so they may have the rose in June.
To this weary world I give a wish that is sincere.
That all men have the right to live in peace instead of fear.
To the folk now old and grey, the ideal for which I fought.
The right to end their closing days in a peace which must be bought.
And now I've given all I own, my life, my dreams, my very whole.
Forgiving all the wrongs I've known, to God I give my soul.

(Written in the AB 64 Pt. 1 of
Corporal John Charles Mills, CMP, in lieu of a Will)

FIRST ANNIVERSARY

Fly again. Fly again, men of the sky,
As you flew that September day, ready to die.
Fight again, fight again, men of the First,
As you fought there at Arnhem, though the Hun did his worst.
Sing again, Sing again, song of the Sten,
Song of the PIAT, the Mills and the Bren.
Fly, fight and sing anniversary night,
Let no man deny you, for freedom's your right.

(Penned by Lcpl Jack Coates in September 1945 on the 1st Anniversary of the Battle of Arnhem.)